Snowbound
With
Mr. Lincoln

President Abraham Lincoln

Taken on April 9, 1865 by Alexander Gardner who managed the Matthew Brady photograph gallery in Washington. This is the last photograph made of Mr. Lincoln. Gardner took 7 pictures of Mr. Lincoln that day. Six were taken on small plates. This one, the last, was taken on a large plate which cracked in handling during the developing process. The crack shows clearly in the developed picture.

Snowbound
With
Mr. Lincoln

JOHN A. LLOYD

VANTAGE PRESS
New York   Washington   Atlanta   Hollywood

Published by Vantage Press, Inc.
516 West 34th Street, New York, New York 10001

Manufactured in the United States of America
Standard Book Number 533-03859-6

Library of Congress Catalog Card No.: 78–060003

Contents

Foreword

Research in preparation for this book began in the spring of 1974 and occupied a great part of the author's time during the next three years. Various interruptions prevented him from beginning the writing until early January 1978. Then a snowfall, the like of which had not been seen in southern Ohio for some forty years, settled over Glendale, Ohio, and two feet of snow covered the landscape for more than a month. He grasped the opportunity to shorten his days at his office and to begin the writing and, during that period, completed most of it.

Thinking constantly for days about Mr. Lincoln and the episodes of his life about which the book is written, the author became so steeped in Lincoln lore that it seemed as though he could almost feel the spirit of Abraham Lincoln.

Hence, the title of the book *Snowbound With Mr. Lincoln*.

It was a great experience.

Acknowledgments

A book may be born in the mind of the author but it requires the talented contribution of many others before it comes into being.

I wish to express my gratitude to Dr. James T. Hickey, librarian and curator of the Abraham Lincoln Library and Museum in Springfield, Illinois, and to Dr. Mark Neely, director of The Louis A. Warren Lincoln Library and Museum in Fort Wayne, Indiana, for their help and criticism; to the staff of Vantage Press, Inc., for their guidance and counsel; to my secretary Mrs. Frederick Schwab for typing the manuscript; to Miss Helen Jones for typing revisions; to Mr. Carl DeLon for assistance in its preparation and to Miss Patricia Inskeep, my executive assistant, for general supervision.

I am especially grateful to Mr. Bruce Catton for permission to quote from "Mr. Lincoln's Army" and to Alfred A. Knopf, Inc., to quote from Mr. T. Harry Williams's work, "Lincoln and His Generals," and to Prof. John S. Goff of Phoenix, Arizona, author of *Robert Todd Lincoln*, a biography of President Lincoln's oldest son, for permission to quote.

Snowbound
With
Mr. Lincoln

Lincoln Defines America

It was August 21, 1864.

The Civil War was at the height of its fury. The battle-weary 166th Ohio regiment, marching through Washington to entrain for a short furlough home, paraded to the president's house (which we now know as the "White House") to pay its respects to the commander-in-chief, President Abraham Lincoln.

There were gaping holes in the roster of the 166th Ohio, deep scars of the toll taken by the enemy, scars of death and wounds and captivity. But their battle flags flew proudly as they marched up Pennsylvania Avenue and on to the lawn of the president's house. They were veteran warriors in their country's cause, and they knew full well that, ere long, they would be in the battle line again facing the same determined Confederate foe.

Only a few of them had seen Mr. Lincoln; fewer had heard his voice, yet he was as familiar to them as their own fathers and brothers. He was a constant, daily subject of conversation, the object of the adverse criticism of some, of the fulsome praise of others; he was the president, the chief magistrate, and their commander-in-chief.

Then, on that humid August day, as they obeyed the command to "halt" in front of the mansion, he appeared. Six feet four inches tall, slightly stooped, his sad eyes mirroring all the horror and woe and grief of war, there he was, and seeing him in the flesh and realizing that he, above everyone else on earth, symbolized the cause for which they fought, they broke into cheers. Their cheers warmed their own hearts

1

and brought a smile to the tired, worried countenance of Abraham Lincoln.

A hush came over the crowd as he began to speak. If they expected a warrior's oration, a resounding denunciation of the enemy, a ringing call to battle and to victory, they may well have been disappointed. For after expressing in simple and sincere words his and the country's appreciation for their heroic services, he turned to a very basic subject: what this awful war is about and what America really is.

I wish it might be more generally and universally understood what the country is now engaged in. We have, as all will agree, a free government where every man has a right to be equal with every other man. In this great struggle this form of government, and every form of human right, is endangered if our enemies succeed. There is involved in this struggle the question of whether your children and my children shall enjoy the privileges we have enjoyed.

I happen, temporarily, to occupy this big, white house. I am a living witness that any one of your children may look to come here as my father's child has. It is in order that each one of you may have, through this free government which we have enjoyed, an open field and a fair chance for your industry, enterprise and intelligence—that you may all have equal privileges in the race of life with all its desirable human aspirations—it is for this that the struggle should be maintained, that we may not lose our birthright. The nation is worth fighting for to secure such an inestimable jewel.

And there you have it: the most succinct, down-to-earth definition of what America is all about that I have been able to find anywhere.

The majority of those in government in our day say that America will have approached the greatness of her goals when we have guaranteed every man an annual wage, whether or not he works for it; when we so mismanage our economy that confusion worse confounded reigns in the marketplace and on the high roads; when we have government doles wasted in the billions every year; when we have a plethora of paper money that loses value with every setting of the sun; when we force business to employ the unfit and slothful; when honest business is hampered by the foolish decrees of arrogant bureaucrats who, although never con-templated in our basic organization of government, now con-stitute a dictatorial menace to all personal freedom. They say it is wonderful that we have a kept people financed by a na-tional debt rising to heights where its weight can collapse the entire economy. And there are all too many who would with joy encourage the proliferation of this bloated economy and this corrupt body politic with more expansive and irre-sponsible welfare programs and the regulations creating socialistic paralysis.

To all of them we must muster the courage to say, "Stop! This is not America. This is not what America should have become! This is not government of the people, by the people, or for the people. Stop and learn. Let Lincoln be your teacher."

For in that short address to those fighting men of the Grand Army, Lincoln defined America, he described the American dream, he illuminated the tapestry of freedom for all to see its grandeur.

Hear him again as we diagram the thoughts revealed in his sentences of November 10, 1864. What is it that he says we have? "A free government where every man has rights." And what are the rights of men under this free government? They constitute, he says "our birthright." What are they?

He lists three:

First, "Every man has a right to be equal with every other man."

Second, "An open field and a fair chance for your indus-try, enterprise and intelligence."

Third, "Equal privileges in the race of life with all its desirable human aspirations."

And that is what America is all about, told simply by one who understood the American dream because he had made it come true for himself and could describe it for every American then and now and forever.

And, indeed, as he said: "The nation is worth fighting for to secure such an inestimable jewel."

Here is no description of freedom producing a "gimme government"; no desire for largess from the tax-filled government trough; no thought of reward without work; of fortune without struggle; of success without toil.

Here is no enthronement of materialism; quite the contrary. Here is the vision of a government that guarantees freedom for the finest ambitions of the human spirit, not for the greedy gratification of 200 million and more gastrointestinal tracts.

Under this, the original concept of America, delineated so clearly by Lincoln, we have the right of all men to be equal with all other men *if,* by their own endeavors, they can achieve equality. In our day we have prostituted this so noble thought by attempting to legislate the equality of all men, and this can no more be done than could Canute compel the tides to do his will. And it should not be done, for the only way man can achieve equality with the best is by his own determined struggle to raise the level of nobility in his own being. There is no other way, and American freedom means to give him the opportunity to achieve that equality, not to wave a magic governmental wand and try to create equality.

Under this original American concept, man is to be secured in his right to "an open field and a fair chance" for his "industry, enterprise and intelligence." And here, indeed, is the glory of the American dream: a fair chance for every man's industry, enterprise, and intelligence. It is exactly because Americans, in days gone by, have grasped this chance that the American dream has come true. But now we discern the point of danger: that government turns its "overpowers" into tyranny and attempts to *control* and to *regulate* and to *circumscribe* man's "industry, enterprise and intelligence." For "overgovernment"—such as we now have—stifles these attributes so necessary to the greatness of a people and their nation.

Finally is the right "that you may all have equal privileges *in the race* of life with all its desirable human aspirations." Not a government-conferred victory in the race of life but "equal privileges in the race"; that is one of the true benefits of liberty.

Such, Lincoln said, is freedom. Such is the purpose of America. "The nation is worth fighting for," he concluded "to secure such an inestimable jewel."

And in that sentence he puts the capsheaf on his definition of America by giving us the challenge of the citizen's duty: to be willing "to fight to secure such an inestimable jewel."

And fight we must, or the robbers will take the jewel.

PART ONE

Before the Presidency

Mr. Lincoln's
Autobiographies

One time before he had been nominated for president, in May 1860, and once afterward, Mr. Lincoln wrote brief autobiographies, the only times in his life when he attempted to put in writing the history of his family or himself.

The first of these two autobiographies was written on December 20, 1859, for Mr. Jesse Wilson Fell, a close personal friend and an influential and active supporter of Mr. Lincoln's campaign in Illinois for delegates to the Republican National Convention to be held the following May.

Fell wrote to Mr. Lincoln asking for a biography, and Lincoln responded as follows:

LETTER TO J. W. FELL

SPRINGFIELD, December 20, 1859.

My dear Sir: Herewith is a little sketch, as you requested. There is not much of it, for the reason, I suppose, that there is not much of me. If anything be made out of it, I wish it to be modest, and not to go beyond the material. If it were thought necessary to incorporate anything from any of my speeches, I suppose there would be no objection. Of course it must not appear to have been written by myself.

Yours very truly,
A. LINCOLN.

AUTOBIOGRAPHY

I was born February 12, 1809, in Hardin County, Kentucky. My parents were both born in Virginia, of undistinguished families—

9

second families, perhaps I should say. My mother, who died in my tenth year, was of a family of the name of Hanks, some of whom now reside in Adams, and others in Macon County, Illinois. My paternal grandfather, Abraham Lincoln, emigrated from Rockingham County, Virginia to Kentucky about 1781 or 1782, where a year or two later he was killed by the Indians, not in battle, but by stealth, when he was laboring to open a farm in the forest. His ancestors, who were Quakers, went to Virginia from Berks County, Pennsylvania. An effort to identify them with the New England family of the same name ended in nothing more definite than a similarity of Christian names in both families, such as Enoch, Levi, Mordecai, Solomon, Abraham, and the like.

My father, at the death of his father, was but six years of age, and he grew up literally without education. He removed from Kentucky to what is now Spencer County, Indiana, in my eighth year. We reached our new home about the time the State came into the Union. It was a wild region, with many bears and other wild animals still in the woods. There I grew up. There were some schools, so called, but no qualification was ever required of a teacher beyond "readin,' writin', and cipherin' " to the rule of three. If a straggler supposed to understand Latin happen to sojourn in the neighborhood, he was looked upon as a wizard. There was absolutely nothing to excite ambition for education. Of course, when I came of age I did not know much. Still, somehow, I could read, write, and cipher to the rule of three, but that was all. I have not been to school since. The little advance I now have upon this store of education, I have picked up from time to time under the pressure of necessity.

I was raised to farm work, which I continued till I was twenty-two. At twenty-one I came to Illinois, Macon County. Then I got to New Salem, at that time in Sangamon, now in Menard County, where I remained a year as a sort of clerk in a store. Then came the Black Hawk war; and I was elected a captain of volunteers, a success which gave me more pleasure than any I have had since. I went the campaign, was elated, ran for the legislature the same year (1832), and was beaten—the only time I ever have been beaten by the people. The next and three succeeding biennial elections I was elected to the legislature. I was not a candidate afterward. During this legislative period I had studied law, and removed to Springfield to practise it. In 1846 I was once elected to the lower House of Congress. Was not a candidate for reëlection. From 1849 to 1854, both inclusive, practised law more assiduously than ever before. Always a Whig in politics; and generally on the Whig electoral tickets, making active canvasses. I was losing interest in politics when the repeal of the Missouri compromise aroused me again. What I have done since then is pretty well known.

If any personal description of me is thought desirable, it may be said I am in height, six feet four inches, nearly: lean in flesh, weighing on an average one hundred and eighty pounds: dark complexion, with coarse black hair and gray eyes. No other marks or brands recollected.

Yours truly,
A. LINCOLN.

The second, written in June of 1860, was for John L. Scripps, a Chicago newspaperman and a member of the journalistic family that founded and still controls Scripps newspapers and radio and television stations. Scripps wrote his "Life of Lincoln," and it was published by the *Chicago Press* and *Tribune* and the *New York Tribune* as "Tribune Tracts No. 6."

The complete text of the autobiography, as written by Mr. Lincoln for Mr. Scripps, follows:

AUTOBIOGRAPHY

Abraham Lincoln was born Feb. 12, 1809, then in Hardin, now in the more recently formed county of Larue, Kentucky. His father, Thomas, & grand-father, Abraham, were born in Rockingham county Virginia, whither their ancestors had come from Berks county Pennsylvania. His lineage has been traced no farther back than this. The family were originally quakers, though in later times they have fallen away from the peculiar habits of that people. The grand-father Abraham, had four brothers—Isaac, Jacob, John & Thomas. So far as known, the descendants of Jacob and John are still in Virginia. Isaac went to a place near where Virginia, North Carolina, and Tennessee, join; and his decendants are in that region. Thomas came to Kentucky, and after many years, died there, whence his decendants went to Missouri. Abraham, grandfather of the subject of this sketch, came to Kentucky, and was killed by indians about the year 1784. He left a widow, three sons and two daughters. The eldest son, Mordecai, remained in Kentucky till late in life, when he removed to Hancock county, Illinois, where soon after he died, and where several of his descendants still reside. The second son, Josiah, removed at an early day to a place on Blue River, now within Harrison [Hancock] county, Indiana; but no recent information of him, or his family, has been obtained. The eldest sister, Mary, married Ralph Crume and some of her descendants are now known to be in Breckenridge county Kentucky. The second sister, Nancy, married William Brumfield, and her family are not known to have left Kentucky, but there is no recent information from them. Thomas, the youngest son, and father of the present subject, by the early death of his father, and very narrow circumstances of his mother, even in childhood was a wandering laboring boy, and grew up litterally without education. He never did more in the way of writing than to bunglingly sign his own name. Before he was grown, he passed one year as a hired hand with his uncle Isaac on Wata[u]ga, a branch of the Holsteen [Holston] River. Getting back into Kentucky, and having reached his 28th. year, he married Nancy Hanks—mother of the present subject—in the year 1806. She also was born in Virginia; and relatives of hers of the name of Hanks, and of other names, now reside in Coles, in Macon, and in Adams counties, Illinois, and also in Iowa. The present subject has no brother or sister of the whole or half blood. He had a sister, older than himself, who was grown and married, but died many years ago, leaving no child. Also a brother, younger than himself, who died in infancy. Before leaving Kentucky he and his sister were sent for short periods, to A.B.C. schools, the first kept by Zachariah Riney, and the second by Caleb Hazel.

At this time his father resided on Knob-creek, on the road from Bardstown Ky. to Nashville Tenn. at a point three, or three and a half miles South or South-West of Atherton's ferry on the Rolling Fork. From this place he removed to what is now Spencer county Indiana, in the autumn of 1816, A. then being in his eight year. This removal was partly on account of slavery; but chiefly on account of the difficulty in land titles in Ky. He settled in an unbroken forest; and the clearing away of surplus wood was the great task a head. A. though very young, was large of his age, and had an axe put into his hands at once; and from that till within his twentythird year, he was almost constantly handling that most useful instrument—less, of course, in plowing and harvesting seasons. At this place A. took an early start as a hunter, which was never much improved afterwards. (A few days before the completion of his eigth year, in the absence of his father, a flock of wild turkeys approached the new log-cabin, and A. with a rifle gun, standing inside, shot through a crack, and killed one of them. He has never since pulled a trigger on any larger game.) In the autumn of 1818 his mother died; and a year afterwards his father married Mrs. Sally Johnston, at Elizabeth-Town, Ky—a widow, with three children of her first marriage. She proved a good and kind mother to A. and is still living in Coles Co. Illinois. There were no children of this second marriage.

His father's residence continued at the same place in Indiana, till 1830. While here A. went to A.B.C. schools by littles, kept successively by Andrew Crawford, —— Sweeney, and Azel W. Dorsey. He does not remember any other. The family of Mr. Dorsey now reside in Schulyer Co. Illinois. A. now thinks that the agregate of all his schooling did not amount to one year. He was never in a college or Academy as a student; and never inside of a college or accademy building till since he had a law-license. What he has in the way of education, he has picked up. After he was twentythree, and had separated from his father, he studied English grammar, imperfectly of course, but so as to speak and write as well as he now does. He studied and nearly mastered the Six-books of Euclid, since he was a member of Congress. He regrets his want of education, and does what he can to supply the want. In his tenth year he was kicked by a horse, and apparantly killed for a time. When he was nineteen, still residing in Indiana, he made his first trip upon a flat/boat to New-Orleans. He was a hired hand merely; and he and a son of the owner, without other assistance, made the trip. The nature of part of the cargo-load, as it was called—made it necessary for them to linger and trade along the Sugar coast—and one night they were attacked by seven negroes with intent to kill and rob them. They were hurt some in the melee, but succeeded in driving the negroes from the boat, and then "cut cable" "weighed anchor" and left.

March 1st. 1830—A. having just completed his 21st year, his father and family, with the families of the two daughters and sons-in-law, of his step-mother, left the old homestead in Indiana, and came to Illinois. Their mode of conveyance was waggons drawn by ox-teams, or A. drove one of the teams. They reached the county of Macon, and stopped there some time within the same month of March. His father and family settled a new place on the North side of the Sangamon river, at the junction of the timber-land and prairie, about ten miles Westerly from Decatur. Here they built a log-cabin, into which they removed, and made sufficient of rails to fence ten acres of ground, fenced and broke the ground, and raised a crop of sow[n] corn upon it the same year. These are, or are supposed to be, the rails about which so much is being said just now, though they are far from being the first, or only rails ever made by A.

The sons-in-law, were temporarily settled at other places in the county. In the autumn all hands were greatly afflicted with augue and fever, to which they had not been used, and by which they were greatly discouraged—so much so that they determined on leaving the county. They remained however, through the succeeding winter, which was the winter of the very celebrated "deep snow" of

Illinois. During that winter, A. together with his step-mother's son, John D. Johnston, and John Hanks, yet residing in Macon county, hired themselves to one Denton Offutt, to take a flat boat from Beardstown Illinois to New-Orleans; and for that purpose, were to join him—Offut—at Springfield, Ills so soon as the snow should go off. When it did go off which was about the 1st. of March 1831—the county was so flooded, as to make traveling by land impracticable; to obviate which difficulty the[y] purchased a large canoe and came down the Sangamon river in it. This is the time and the manner of A's first entrance into Sangamon County. They found Offutt at Springfield, but learned from him that he had failed in getting a boat at Beardstown. This lead to their hiring themselves to him at $12 per month, each; and getting the timber out of the trees and building a boat at old Sangamon Town on the Sangamon river, seven miles N.W. of Springfield, which boat they took to New-Orleans, substantially upon the old contract. It was in connection with this boat that occurred the ludicrous incident of sewing up the hogs eyes. Offutt bought thirty odd large fat live hogs, but found difficulty in driving them from where [he] purchased them to the boat, and thereupon conceived the whim that he could sew up their eyes and drive them where he pleased. No sooner thought of than decided, he put his hands, including A. at the job, which they completed—all but the driving. In their blind condition they could not be driven out of the lot or field they were in. This expedient failing, they were tied and hauled on carts to the boat. It was near the Sangamon River, within what is now Menard county.

During this boat enterprize acquaintance with Offutt, who was previously an entire stranger, he conceved a liking for A. and believing he could turn him to account, he contracted with him to act as clerk for him, on his return from New-Orleans, in charge of a store and Mill at New-Salem, then in Sangamon, now in Menard county. Hanks had not gone to New-Orleans, but having a family, and being likely to be detained from home longer than at first expected, had turned back from St. Louis. He is the same John Hanks who now engineers the "rail enterprize" at Decatur; and is a first cousin to A's mother. A's father, with his own family & others mentioned, had, in pursuance of their intention, removed from Macon to Coles county. John D. Johnston, the step-mother's son, went to them; and A. stopped indefinitely, and, for the first time, as it were, by himself at New-Salem, before mentioned. This was in July 1831. Here he rapidly made acquaintances and friends. In less than a year Offutt's business was failing—had almost failed—when the Black-Hawk war of 1832—broke out. A joined a volunteer company, and to his own surprize, was elected captain of it. He says he has not since had any success in life which gave him so much satisfaction. He went the campaign, served near three months, met the ordinary hardships of such an expedition, but was in no battle. He now owns in Iowa, the land upon which his own warrants for this service, were located. Returning from the campaign, and encouraged by his great popularity among his immediate neighbors, he, the same year, ran for the Legislature and was beaten—his own precinct, however, casting it's votes 277 for and 7, against him. And this too while he was an avowed Clay man, and the precinct the autumn afterwards, giving a majority of 115 to Genl. Jackson over Mr. Clay. This was the only time A was ever beaten on a direct vote of the people. He was now without means and out of business, but was anxious to remain with his friends who had treated him with so much generosity, especially as he had nothing elsewhere to go to. He studied what he should do—thought of learning the black-smith trade—thought of trying to study law—rather thought he could not succeed at that without a better education. Before long, strangely enough, a man offered to sell and did sell, to A. and another as poor as himself, an old stock of goods, upon credit. They opened as merchants; and he says that was the store. Of course they did nothing but get deeper and deeper in debt. He was appointed Postmaster at New-Salem—the office being too insignificant, to make his politics an objection. The store winked out. The Surveyor of Sangamon, offered to depute to A that portion of his work which was within his part of the county. He accepted, procured a compass and chain, studied Flint, and Gibson a little, and went at it. This procured bread, and kept soul and body together. The election of 1834 came, and he was then elected to the Legislature by the highest vote cast for any candidate. Major John T. Stuart, then in full practice of the law, was also elected. During the canvass, in a private conversation he encouraged A. [to] study law. After the election he borrowed books of Stuart, took them home with him, and went at it in good earnest. He studied with nobody. He still mixed in the surveying to pay board and clothing bills. When the Legislature met, the law books were dropped, but were taken up again at the end of the session. He was re-elected in 1836, 1838, and 1840. In the autumn of 1836 he obtained a law licence, and on April 15, 1837 removed to Springfield, and commenced the practice, his old friend, Stuart taking him into partnership. March 3rd. 1837, by a protest entered upon the Ills. House Journal of that date, at pages 817, 818, A. with Dan Stone, another representative of Sangamon, briefly defined his position on the slavery question; and so far as it goes, it was then the same that it is now. The protest is as follows—(Here insert it) In 1838, & 1840 Mr. L's party in the Legislature voted for him as Speaker; but being

15

in the minority, he was not elected. After 1840 he declined a re-election to the Legislature. He was on the Harrison electoral ticket in 1840, and on that of Clay in 1844, and spent much time and labor in both those canvasses. In Nov. 1842 he was married to Mary, daughter of Robert S. Todd, of Lexington, Kentucky. They have three living children, all sons—one born in 1843, one in 1850, and one in 1853. They lost one, who was born in 1846. In 1846, he was elected to the lower House of Congress, and served one term only, commencing in Dec. 1847 and ending with the inauguration of Gen. Taylor, in March 1849. All the battles of the Mexican war had been fought before Mr. L. took his seat in congress, but the American army was still in Mexico, and the treaty of peace was not fully and formally ratified till the June afterwards. Much has been said of his course in Congress in regard to this war. A careful examination of the Journals and Congressional Globe shows, that he voted for all the supply measures which came up, and for all the measures in any way favorable to the officers, soldiers, and their families, who conducted the war through; with this exception that some of these measures passed without yeas and nays, leaving no record as to how particular men voted. The Journals and Globe also show him voting that the war was unnecessarily and unconstitutionally begun by the President of the United States. This is the language of Mr. Ashmun's amendment, for which Mr. L. and nearly or quite all, other whigs of the H. R. voted.

Mr. L's reasons for the opinion expressed by this vote were briefly that the President had sent Genl. Taylor into an inhabited part of the country belonging to Mexico, and not to the U.S. and thereby had provoked the first act of hostility—in fact the commencement of the war; that the place, being the country bordering on the East bank of the Rio Grande, was inhabited by native Mexicans, born there under the Mexican government; and had never submitted to, nor been conquered by Texas, or the U.S. nor transferred to either by treaty—that although Texas claimed the Rio Grande as her boundary, Mexico had never recognized it, the people on the ground had never recognized it, and neither Texas nor the U.S. had ever enforced it—that there was a broad desert between that, and the country over which Texas had actual control—that the country where hostilities commenced, having once belonged to Mexico, must remain so, until it was somehow legally transferred, which had never been done.

Mr. L. thought the act of sending an armed force among the Mexicans, was *unnecessary*, inasmuch as Mexico was in no way molesting, or menacing the U.S. or the people thereof; and that it was *unconstitutional*, because the power of levying war is vested in

Congress, and not in the President. He thought the principal motive for the act, was to divert public attention from the surrender of "Fifty-four, forty, or fight" to Great Brittain, on the Oregon boundary question.

Mr. L. was not a candidate for re-election. This was determined upon, and declared before he went to Washington, in accordance with an understanding among whig friends, by which Col. Hardin, and Col. Baker had each previously served a single term in the same District.

In 1848, during his term in congress, he advocated Gen. Taylor's nomination for the Presidency, in opposition to all others, and also took an active part for his election, after his nomination— speaking a few times in Maryland, near Washington, several times in Massachusetts, and canvassing quite fully his own district in Illinois, which was followed by a majority in the district of over 1500 for Gen. Taylor.

Upon his return from Congress he went to the practice of the law with greater earnestness than ever before. In 1852 he was upon the Scott electoral ticket, and did something in the way of canvassing. but owing to the hopelessness of the cause in Illinois, he did less than in previous presidential canvasses.

In 1854, his profession had almost superseded the thought of politics in his mind, when the repeal of the Missouri compromise aroused him as he had never been before.

In the autumn of that year he took the stump with no broader practical aim or object that [than?] to secure, if possible, the reelection of Hon Richard Yates to congress. His speeches at once attracted a more marked attention than they had ever before done. As the canvass proceeded, he was drawn to different parts of the state, outside of Mr. Yates' district. He did not abandon the law, but gave his attention, by turns, to that and politics. The State agricultural fair was at Springfield that year, and Douglas was announced to speak there.

In the canvass of 1856, Mr. L. made over fifty speeches, no one of which, so far as he remembers, was put in print. One of them was made at Galena, but Mr. L. has no recollection of any part of it being printed; nor does he remember whether in that speech he said anything about a Supreme court decision. He may have spoken upon that subject; and some of the newspapers may have reported him as saying what is now ascribed to him; but he thinks he could not have expressed himself as represented.

Residences of the Lincolns

On November 4, 1842, the newly wed Abraham and Mary Todd Lincoln moved into a suite of rooms in Globe Tavern and set up housekeeping there. Two of Mary's sisters had begun their married life in this same suite of rooms, each couple later moving into houses when children began to arrive. In starting their married life in the Globe, the Lincolns were following tradition in the Todd family.

The Lincolns lived in the hotel from the day of their marriage until about mid-November 1843, when they moved into a small, rented house on the east side of Fourth Street between Adams and Monroe. Rumor has it that baby Robert's cries disturbed other lodgers in the tavern, but the probability is that the birth of his son on August 1, 1843, made more ample quarters than a two-room hotel suite a necessity.

On May 10, 1843, Mr. Lincoln wrote to his friend, Joshua F. Speed: "We are not keeping house; but boarding at the Globe Tavern which is very well kept by a widow lady name of Beck. Our room (the same as Dr. Wallace occupied there) and boarding costs four dollars a week."

Even while making this move, the Lincolns were seeking a still more suitable residence, and on January 16, 1844, Mr. Lincoln entered into a contract to purchase the house at Eighth and Jackson streets which was to be his home until he left for Washington in 1861 to assume the presidency. It was a story-and-a-half house with stable. The house was five years old and belonged to the Rev'd. Charles Dresser, the Episcopal rector in Springfield, a close friend of Lincoln's. Mr. Dresser was the clergyman who had officiated at the Lincoln wedding.

The price of the house was $1,500, $750 of which was paid when the contract was signed and the balance, $750, on February 15, 1844. The second $750 included funds secured by Mr. Lincoln from the sale of two lots located near the home he purchased, property that he had owned for some time. At the time he purchased the house, Mr. Lincoln owned four lots in the same neighborhood, two of them across the street. One of them is the lot where a Lincoln Museum now is located, directly across from the Lincoln property.

In 1855, the Lincolns enlarged their house by converting the "half story" into a full second floor. This addition and remodeling cost Mr. Lincoln $1,300.

The property was clear of debt throughout Mr. Lincoln's ownership.

From the time they moved into their new home, the Lincolns always had housekeeping help in the form of "hired girls" who "lived in."

Mrs. Lincoln was a fine seamstress and a good cook. She was an accomplished hostess and a woman of unusually good education for the times in which she lived; she was knowledgeable about political and civic affairs and active in the social life of the community. She was a member of the Presbyterian church.

Mr. Lincoln's So-Called
Favorite Poem

Much has been written about a poem entitled "Oh, why should the spirit of mortal be proud," which is alleged to have been Mr. Lincoln's "favorite" poem.

This whimsical six-verse poem first appears in Lincoln literature in a eulogy of President Zachary Taylor that Congressman Lincoln delivered in the House of Representatives on July 25, 1850. General Taylor, hero of the Mexican War, was elected twelfth president of the United States in 1848, defeating Lewis Cass and Martin Van Buren, who had served as president from 1837 to 1841. Taylor died of typhus on July 9, 1850, after serving but one year of his term. He was succeeded by Vice President Millard Fillmore.

Congressman Lincoln, prominent among the Whigs in the House, was chosen to deliver a eulogy on the life of President Taylor. He concluded his address with this paragraph commenting on death and with the poem:

... his labor, his name, his memory and example, are all that is left us—his example, verifying the great truth, that "he that humbleth himself, shall be exalted" teaching, that to serve one's country with a singleness of purpose, gives assurance of that country's gratitude, secures its best honors, and makes "a dying bed, soft as downy pillows are."

The death of the late President may not be without its use, in reminding us, that *we* too, must die. Death, abstractly considered, is the same with the high as with the low; but practically, we are not so much aroused to the contemplation of our own mortal natures, by the fall of *many* undistinguished, as that of *one* great, and well known, name. By the latter, we are forced to muse, and ponder, sadly.

Oh, why should the spirit of mortal be proud

So the multitude goes, like the flower or the weed,
That withers away to let others succeed;
So the multitude comes, even those we behold,
To repeat every tale that has often been told.

For we are the same, our father have been,
We see the same sights our fathers have seen;
We drink the same streams and see the same sun
And run the same course our fathers have run.

They loved; but the story we cannot unfold;
They scorned, but the heart of the haughty is cold;
They grieved, but no wail from their slumbers will come,
They joyed, but the tongue of their gladness is dumb.

They died! Aye, they died; we things that are now;
That work on the turf that lies on their brow,
And make in their dwellings a transient abode,
Meet the things that they met on their pilgrimage road.

Yea! hope and despondency, pleasure and pain,
Are mingled together in sun-shine and rain;
And the smile and the tear, and the song and the dirge,
Still follow each other, like surge upon surge.

'Tis the wink of an eye, 'tis the draught of a breath,
From the blossoms of health, to the paleness of death.
From the gilded saloon, to the bier and the shroud.
Oh, why should the spirit of mortal be proud!

Whether this was Mr. Lincoln's "favorite" poem is difficult to determine. He is alleged to have quoted it frequently, but such is not clearly documented to my satisfaction.

One must admit, however, that viewing life as it is and as it ever has been, this is a good question: "Oh, why should the spirit of mortal be proud?"

21

Lincoln, the "Law School" Teacher

Abraham Lincoln began to study law in 1834 during his second campaign for the legislature. His mentor was a friend, John T. Stuart, a prosperous and prominent Springfield lawyer who shared a room with Lincoln in Vandalia (then the capital of Illinois) while the legislature was in progress. Stuart furnished Lincoln the lawbooks necessary for his study, and on March 24, 1836, Lincoln, age twenty-five, was certified by the Sangamon Circuit Court as "a person of good moral character." Such certification was the first requirement for admission to the bar.

On September 9, 1836, young Lincoln took and passed his bar examination, appearing before the bar examiners and submitting to an oral examination. He received his license, and later that day, as was the custom, he treated his examiners to dinner. Passing the examination was the second step.

Enrollment on the list of licensed lawyers was the third step, and that came two days later. On September 11, 1836, Abraham Lincoln was enrolled as a lawyer by the Clerk of the Supreme Court of Illinois.

Immediately, he began to practice with the firm of Stuart and Dummer, and shortly thereafter, when Mr. Henry E. Dummer moved to Beardstown, Lincoln replaced him as a partner, and the firm became Stuart and Lincoln.

In the spring of 1841, Messrs. Stuart and Lincoln "reached an amicable parting of the ways and Lincoln formed a new partnership with Stephen T. Logan."

Logan was recognized as one of the leading lawyers in Illinois. That he took Lincoln into partnership on a fifty-fifty basis indicates that lawyer Lincoln in a short time had developed an enviable reputation for a young practitioner of a difficult profession.

Logan was a perfectionist. He insisted on thorough research and well and precisely written pleadings, briefs, and other documents. His impact on Lincoln was to convert his protégé into the same kind of thorough practitioner. As a result, Lincoln, throughout his lifetime, insisted on thorough research and clearly written documents and worked and studied constantly to improve his ability to express himself accurately both orally and in writing. Out of this training, inspired by Logan, grew the great master who could produce the Gettysburg Address and the first and second inaugurals.

Logan and Lincoln trained many young men for the law. These students worked in their offices while carrying on their studies and preparing for their examinations.

Portrait and Biographical Record of Tazewell and Mason Counties, Illinois, published by Biographical Publishing Company, Chicago, in 1894, is a biography of a celebrated lawyer named Benjamin S. Pretzinger in which this paragraph, giving a hint of the teaching activity of the Logan and Lincoln firm, occurs:

In 1844, Pretzinger, desiring to begin the study of law, "went to the office of Logan and Lincoln, but it was *crowded* with law students, and Logan advised him to get some legal books, adding that he would loan him such volumes as he desired."

Young Pretzinger took his advice and studied with success.

NOTES FOR A LAW LECTURE

In the *Collected Works of Abraham Lincoln,* Volume II, is the text of "Fragmented Notes for a Law Lecture," which bear the date July 1, 1850, in parenthesis, the date marked with a question mark. The question is not whether the "Notes" are authentic but that the month and day may not be accurate.

The following is the text of the notes for the lecture attorney Lincoln planned to deliver to law students and prospective students. It occurs to me that they are as applicable in 1978 as they were in 1850, which illuminates one facet of Mr. Lincoln's character. He based his life on permanent values and judged all of his actions thereby, never changing principles to serve expediency.

I am not an accomplished lawyer. I find quite as much material for a lecture, in those points wherein I have failed, as in those wherein I have been moderately successful.

The leading rule for the lawyer, as for the man, of every calling, is *diligence*. Leave nothing for tomorrow, which can be done today. Never let your correspondence fall behind. Whatever piece of business you have in hand, before stopping, do all the labor pertaining to it which can then be done. When you bring a common-law suit, if you have the facts for doing so, write the declaration at once. If a law point be involved, examine the books, and note the authority you rely on, upon the declaration itself, where you are sure to find it when wanted. The same of defenses and pleas. In business not likely to be litigated—ordinary collection cases, foreclosures, partitions, and the like,—make all examinations of titles and note them and even draft orders and decrees in advance. This course has tripple advantage; it avoids omissions and neglect; saves your labor, when once done; performs the labor out of court when you have leisure rather than in court when you have not. Extemporaneous speaking should be practiced and cultivated. It is the lawyer's avenue to the public. However able and faithful he may be in other respects, people are slow to bring him business, if he cannot make a speech. And yet there is not a more fatal error to young lawyers, than relying too much on speech-making. If any one, upon his rare powers of speaking, shall claim exemption from the drudgery of the law, his case is a failure in advance.

Discourage litigation. Persuade your neighbors to compromise whenever you can. Point out to them how the nominal winner is often a real loser—in fees, and expenses, and waste of time. As a peace-maker the lawyer has a superior opertunity of being a good man. There will still be business enough.

Never stir up litigation. A worse man can scarcely be found than one who does this. Who can be more nearly a fiend than he who habitually overhauls the Register of deeds, in search of defects in titles whereon to stir up strife, and put money in his pocket? A moral tone ought to be infused into the profession, which should drive such men out of it.

The matter of fees is important far beyond the mere question of bread and butter involved. Properly attended to fuller justice is done to both lawyer and client. An exorbitant fee should never be claimed. As a general rule, never take your whole fee in advance, nor any more than a small retainer. When fully paid beforehand, you are more than a common mortal if you can feel the same interest in the case, as if something was still in prospect for you, as well as for your client. And when you lack interest in the case the job will very likely lack skill and diligence in the performance. Settle the amount of fee, and take a note in advance. Then you will feel that you are working for something, and you are sure to do your work faithfully and well. Never sell a fee-note—at least, not before the consideration service is performed. It leads to negligence and dishonesty, by losing interest in the case, and dishonesty in refusing to refund, when you have allowed the consideration to fail.

There is a vague popular belief that lawyers are necessarily dishonest. I say vague, because when we consider to what extent confidence, and honors are reposed in, and conferred upon lawyers by the people, it appears improbable that their impression of dishonesty is very distinct and vivid. Yet the impression, in common—almost universal. Let no young man, choosing the law for a calling, for a moment yield to this popular belief. Resolve to be honest at all events; and if, in your own judgment, you can not be an honest lawyer, resolve to be honest without being a lawyer. Choose some other occupation, rather than one in the choosing of which you do, in advance, consent to be a knave.

"WORK, WORK, WORK IS THE MAIN THING"

During the presidential campaign of 1860, a young schoolteacher named J. M. Brockman of Pleasant Plains, Illinois, wrote to Mr. Lincoln asking how to become a lawyer. Lincoln's answer is very interesting. He wrote to Brockman as follows on September 25, 1860:

9/25/1860

J.M.Brockman, Esq.
Pleasant Plains, Ill.

Dear Sir—Yours of the 24th asking "the best mode of obtaining a thorough knowledge of the law" is received. The mode is very simple, though laborious and tedious. It is only to get the books and read and study them carefully. Begin with Blackstone's Commentaries and after reading it carefully through, say twice, take up Chittey's pleading. Greenleaf's Evidence and Story's Equity etc. in succession. Work, work, work is the main thing.

Yours very truly,
A. Lincoln

Brockman later responded to the call of President Lincoln for troops and served in the Fifth Iowa Cavalry. After the war, he settled in Nebraska, became a farmer and stockman, and entered politics. He served two terms in the Nebraska legislature. But he never became a lawyer!

Mr. Lincoln's letter, written when he was right in the busy midst of his campaign for the presidency, indicates that his interest in helping young men who aspired to become lawyers never waned. It would have been normal for a presidential candidate to have a secretary respond to such a letter with something like "Mr. Lincoln directs me to tell you to do this, etc."

But Mr. Lincoln was interested in ambitious young people, interested enough to take the time to write in his own hand and give this young man the best advice he could.

Medical Malpractice Case

To physicians and practitioners in other professions who think the malpractice suit is a development of this era, it should be said, "'Tain't so." There is a greatly increased number of such suits in this day and age, but this sort of litigation has been going on for many years.

As an instance, there is the case of *Samuel Fleming* v. *Eli Crothers and Thomas P. Rogers*, filed on March 28, 1856, in the Circuit Court of McLean County, Illinois.

The alleged malpractice took place in Bloomington, Illinois, and the defendant-physicians hired legal counsel to represent them. Local counsel decided that the case was beyond their experience and that they needed a lawyer with more expertise. They turned to Abraham Lincoln, and he took charge of the defense.

While Drs. Crothers and Rogers were named as defendants, Dr. Jacob R. Freese, who also had attended the patient, had moved, subsequent to the incident, to Cincinnati, and the plaintiff did not make him a party to the suit.

I have in my possession a photocopy of all the pleadings in the case, all handwritten, one of the documents in Mr. Lincoln's handwriting. The originals are in the Museum of the Lincoln Memorial University of Harrogate, Tennessee, and Edgar G. Archer, museum conservator, very kindly arranged for me to have them photographed.

Fleming had been a spectator at a fire in the livery stable back of the Morgan House (a hotel) in Bloomington on the night of October 16, 1855. Before it could be extinguished, one man, William Green, a drayman, had been killed, and Fleming, who was a carpenter, was injured when struck by debris from the Morgan House chimney when it fell. The

27

blaze not only destroyed the livery stable but consumed also the hotel and all but two buildings in the block where the fire broke out.

Relatives moved Fleming to the home of his brother, where Drs. Crothers, Freese, and Rogers attended him. The physicians determined that both of Fleming's legs were broken, and the doctors bound them with splints. One version refers to fractures in the thighs, but others use the word "legs." All agree that he was very seriously injured.

Fleming was making a good recovery, and the doctors removed the splints in three weeks. It was then found that while the left leg was straight, the right leg was crooked. Upon observing the situation, the doctors proposed that they break Fleming's leg and reset it. To this Fleming agreed.

As the surgery started, Isaac M. Small, a young man studying medicine under the preceptorship of Dr. Rogers, administered chloroform as an anesthetic, and Dr. Rogers began pulling on the leg to break the adhesions. Apparently the chloroform had not been given in an amount sufficient to effect anesthesia because Fleming began to cry out from the pain. One account says that he "screamed and cried out, 'Hold on, hold on,' declaring that he would rather have a crooked leg than undergo such pain."

Dr. Crothers explained to him that unless he permitted them to continue with the operation and straighten the leg, it would always be crooked. Fleming insisted that he "leave it alone," and his relatives who were present agreed with the patient. So the physicians stopped the process of breaking and resetting the leg.

The leg healed but it was "misshaped and crooked" as the doctor had predicted.

Fleming sued. The charge in the petition alleges that the physicians undertook to return his legs to normal function and then reads "yet the said defendants not regarding said duty but intending and contriving to injure the said plaintiff in this respect did not or would not use due and proper care, skill or diligence in and about the endeavoring to cure the said plaintiff of the said malady and illness aforesaid, to wit his broken legs aforesaid, but on the contrary thereof the said defendants then and there conducted themselves in an ignorant, unskilful and negligent manner in that behalf. By reason of which said premises the said plaintiff became and was and still is greatly injured and prejudiced in his health and constitution," etc.

The complaint goes on for a great many more words, including an amazing number of "saids" and "aforesaids," etc. and prays for $10,000 damages from the two physicians.

Fleming's lawyers were Leonard Swett and William Ward Orme, William H. Hanna and John W. Scott, and Asahel Gridley and John H. Wickizer.

Defendants' lawyers were Abraham Lincoln and John T. Stuart and David Brier and Jesse Birch and L. L. Strain and Andrew W. Rogers, the latter two firms being located in Bloomington.

It was a year from the time the suit was filed and the battle lines drawn that the case went to trial with Judge David Davis on the bench. Mr. Lincoln carried the laboring oar for the defendants. In the days before trial, he prepared himself carefully on the anatomical aspects of the case and worked with Dr. Crothers as well as spending hours in the library. One of the matters he wanted to get before the jury was the chemistry of the growth of bones and the changes that occur in bone structure and other organic matter brought on by advancing age; how among older people bones become brittle. The point was important because Fleming was a middle-aged man.

To get this physiological fact over to the jury, Mr. Lincoln secured chicken bones—some from young and some from old chickens—and used them to demonstrate his point. He was successful.

In cross-examining Fleming, he held up the older bone, commenting in language the jury could understand, "This bone has the strength all taken out of it." "Can you walk at all?" Lincoln asked Fleming. "Yes, but my leg is short so I have to limp." Whereupon Lincoln commented: "Well, what I would advise you to do is to get down on your knees and thank your Heavenly Father and also these two doctors that you have any legs to stand on at all."

It took a week to try the case, in which twenty-seven doctors testified, some on one side and some on the other.

The jury was out eighteen hours and could not reach a verdict, so Judge Davis dismissed the jurors and ordered the case retried at the next term of court.

Before the retrial could begin, the plaintiff tossed in the

towel. Both parties agreed to the dismissal of the case, defendants to pay "the fee bill issued against them" and that "the suit be dismissed at the cost of the Plaintiff."

Swett signed the order for the plaintiff and Brier for the defendants.

So did Lincoln win for his doctor clients.

So far as is known, the case had no impact on the present rapidly rising cost of medical malpractice insurance.

Here is a photograph of one of the pleadings in the malpractice case. It is in Mr. Lincoln's handwriting and permission to publish it is granted by Dr. James T. Hickey, Curator of the Abraham Lincoln Library and Museum in Springfield, Illinois. The original is Dr. Hickey's personal property.

"I Will Pay It If It Is Right; But I Do Not Wish to Be 'Diddled' "

On September 17, 1859, Abraham Lincoln came to Cincinnati as the guest of the Republican party and delivered a major political address. The incident received national publicity. Mr. Lincoln made three major political speeches in Ohio that month, one in Columbus on the sixteenth, one in Dayton, and another in Cincinnati on the seventeenth.

Subsequently, a most interesting incident developed concerning his hotel bill at the Burnet House, which at that time was Cincinnati's leading hotel, located at the corner of Vine and Third streets. The hotel was torn down about 1926 to make room for a large annex to the main building of the Union Central Life Insurance Company's home office at Fourth and Vine streets. Union Central occupied both buildings until 1964, when it moved to its present location in the northern part of Hamilton County. The building on the site of the Burnet House now is called the Central Trust Annex.

Mr. Lincoln was accompanied by Mrs. Lincoln and one of their sons, whom he describes as "one small child."

The Republican committee was responsible for paying the Lincolns' hotel bill and failed to do so. As a result, on June 15, 1860, the hotel wrote to Mr. Lincoln a very apologetic letter reciting that "it appears that there is no remedy left us other than to advise you of its never having been paid."

Upon receipt of the letter from Johnson, Saunders and Company, which operated the hotel, Mr. Lincoln wrote on June 7, 1860, to the Hon. W. M. Dickson, who was the chairman of the Republican committee in Cincinnati, as follows:

31

Springfield, Ill. June 7, 1860

Hon. W. M. Dickson

My dear Sir:

Your telegraphic despatch, the day of the nomination, was received; as also was, in due course, your kind letter of May 21st with Cousin Annie's note at the end of it.

I have just now received a letter from Cincinnati, of which the following is a copy:

"Cincinnati, June 5, 1860.

Hon. A. Lincoln

Dr. Sir:

We are extremely sorry to be under the necessity of calling your attention to the enclosed bill during your sojourn at the Burnet in Sept. last; but it appears there is no remedy left us other than to advise you of its never having been paid. We relied upon the Republican Committee, but as yet have not been able to find anyone being willing to take the responsibility of paying same—consequently advise you in the premises.

Very respectfully yours,

Johnson, Saunders & Co."

The enclosed bill is as follows:

"Burnet House

Cincinnati. Sept. 19, 1859.

Hon. A. Lincoln

To Johnson, Saunders & Company, Dr.

Board and Parlor self and family	37.50
Extra suppers 3.50; wines, liquors and cigars 7.50	11.00

Occupancy of room no. 15 Committee   5.00

$53.50"

Now this may be right, but I have a slight suspicion of it, for two or three reasons. First, when I left, I called at the office of the Hotel, and was then distinctly told the bill "was settled" "was all right" or words to that effect. Secondly, it seems a little steep that "Board and parlor from Saturday 7-1/2 p.m. to Monday 10-1/2 A.M. for a man, woman and one small child, should be $37.50. Thirdly, we had no extra suppers, unless having tea at our room the first evening, was such. We were in the house over the time of five meals, three only of which we took in the house. We did not once dine in the house. As to wines, liquors and cigars, we had none—absolutely none. These last may have been in room 15 by order of Committee, but I do not recollect them at all.

Please look into this, and write me. I can and will pay it if it is right; but I do not wish to be "diddled!" Please do what you do quietly, having no fuss about it.

Yours very truly,
A Lincoln.

The Committee "passed the hat" and paid the bill.
Mr. Lincoln got his "wish." He wasn't "diddled."

Spending Election Day, 1860, With Mr. Lincoln

On Tuesday, November 5, 1860, Abraham Lincoln visited the post office in Springfield, Illinois, to get his mail. A bystander asked him how he intended to vote. Mr. Lincoln, who was the Republican nominee for president at the general election to be held that day, replied: "For Yates for Governor." "But for president, how vote?" the bystander insisted. "By ballot!" Lincoln replied, and walked away, his arms full of mail.

About three o'clock that afternoon, Mr. Lincoln walked to his precinct polling place after having spent most of the day in his temporary office in the State House. The voting booth was in the court house nearby. A crowd of friends and neighbors had gathered, and they gave him a tremendous ovation as he walked in to cast his vote. He secured his ballot, cut the names of his own electors from it, then voted a straight Republican ticket, deposited it in the box, and returned to his office. By the device of cutting off the names of the presidential electors Mr. Lincoln did not vote for himself for president, apparently feeling that a candidate should not vote for himself. The crowd cheered him every step of that significant journey.

Mr. Lincoln spent the evening in the telegraph office getting returns. The result was not long in doubt. The telegraph instrument clicked off the results steadily, and by about eleven o'clock, Mr. Lincoln knew that he had been elected to be the sixteenth president of the United States.

Assured of victory, he walked the few blocks from the

telegraph office to his home to tell Mrs. Lincoln the news. It was shortly after eleven o'clock. He lay down on a sofa to rest a few minutes; then, a little after midnight, he and Mrs. Lincoln attended a supper with friends and soon thereafter went home, a weary but very happy couple. Mr. Lincoln had received one hundred and eighty electoral votes; John C. Breckenridge, seventy-two; John Bell, thirty-nine and Stephen A. Douglas, twelve.

The next morning, Mr. Lincoln was back at work in his office That evening, he attended a "victory celebration" and listened to speeches but declined to give one.

Suddenly, life changed dramatically for Abraham Lincoln. The Springfield lawyer was president-elect of the United States, due to assume that office on March 4, 1861.

The entire country was in turmoil. Soon Southern states would begin their attempt to secede from the Union. A new political party had won and there was the question of how the president-elect would handle patronage.

A cabinet must be selected and powerful politicians and their supporters were bringing heavy pressure on the victorious candidate.

A myriad of seekers of offices and jobs, both major and minor, began to besiege him.

Mail arrived in huge amounts. Much of it was important; much trivial. All of it had to be dealt with, most had to be answered.

There was no huge governmentally provided fund such as we have today, to finance the transitionary period from election to assumption of office. The successful candidate must provide staff and other costly necessities out of his own pocket.

So, hectically, began the interim months between November 5, 1860 and March 4, 1861, for Abraham and Mary Lincoln, and their children.

It was a "new world" and every eye was on them.

Begins Journey to Destiny

By February 11, 1861, the interim chores were done and Abraham Lincoln boarded a special train at the depot in Springfield and began the long journey to meet his destiny.

The morning of February 11, 1861, the day he started for Washington for his first inauguration, Lincoln, himself, roped all of his family's trunks and tagged each one: "A. Lincoln, White House, Washington, D.C." Then he was driven to the railroad station.

About 1,000 people, friends and neighbors, gathered to bid him "good-by." It was an emotion-charged gathering. Their friend was leaving to assume the highest position in the entire country. They were very proud of him. They knew they would miss him, and they knew what lay ahead—crisis, trouble, maybe war.

To them, he spoke in beautiful simplicity what was in his mind and heart.

No one, not in my situation, can appreciate my feeling of sadness at this parting. To this place, and the kindness of these people, I owe everything. Here I have lived for a quarter of a century and have passed from a young man to an old man. Here my children have been born, and one is buried. I now leave, not knowing when, or whether ever, I may return, with a task before me greater than that which rested upon Washington. Without the assistance of that Divine Being who ever attended him I cannot succeed. With that assistance I cannot fail. Trusting in Him who can go with me and remain with you and be everywhere for good, let us confidently hope that all will yet be well. To His care commending you, as I hope in your prayers you will commend me, I bid you an affectionate farewell.

And so he left home and friends and cherished associations, that great, simple, uncomplicated man, to assume his seemingly impossible task.

Working at that task, day by day from dawn's first light to midnight's sinister hour, with the same simplicity, humility, honor, and honesty and directness that had characterized his life in Springfield, through four years and a month and a half, he did his chores for the people.

And, likewise, as Lincoln toiled, He who could go with him did so and with "that assistance" he did not fail. Our united country was saved. His leadership saved it.

More than a hundred years have passed since an assassin's bullet struck him down, and in that century and more the country that he saved became the mightiest nation on earth. Now, again, she has fallen upon evil days. I can find only one clear certainty in our era of crisis and trouble. I get it from Lincoln, speaking on the day he left home, to take up his great burden of sorrow: "without that assistance from Him who can be with me and remain with you and be everywhere for good we cannot succeed. With it, we cannot fail."

PART TWO

The Presidency

One Day in the Life of
President Lincoln

On Monday, February 8, 1865, Abraham Lincoln, president of the United States, rose at 5:30 in the morning. By a little after six, he had left his bedroom in the west wing of the second floor of the White House and gone directly to his office on the same floor in the east wing.

Mr. Lincoln's office was a large room, facing south and was next to the office of John G. Nicolay, his principal secretary, which was in the southeast corner. Its furnishings were simple: a large oak table, covered with cloth, around which the Cabinet met; another table between the two long windows at which Lincoln, seated in a large armchair, usually did his writing. A tall desk with pigeonholes for papers stood against the south wall. A few straight-back chairs and two plain black horsehair-covered sofas completed the furnishings. There was a bell cord near the president's desk.

A marble mantel surmounted the fireplace with its high brass fender and brass andirons. Glass-globed gas jets hung from the ceiling. An old, discolored engraving of President Jackson hung above the mantel. A photograph of John Bright, the English liberal leader, and a number of military maps in wooden frames completed the wall decorations. One door opened into Nicolay's office and another into the hall. A messenger, whose duty it was to bring in the cards of visitors, was stationed by the entrance from the hall.

John Hay, one of Mr. Lincoln's secretaries, acknowledged some of the president's mail, usually with the introduction: "In reply to your letter, the President directs me to say—";

but where an answer was required, Lincoln, himself, composed and wrote it.

The filing system was the same kind that had served him as a country lawyer. The pigeonholes of his tall desk were marked alphabetically, with a few of the apertures assigned to individuals. There was one for each cabinet member and one for each of a number of generals. There was one for Horace Greeley, and then there was a compartment marked "W. & W." This, it is said, aroused the interest of Frank B. Carpenter, the artist, and Lincoln explained: "That's Weed and Wood—Thurlow and Fernandy." "That's a pair of 'em," he chuckled. Thurlow Weed, you will remember, was a New York political figure, and Fernando Wood was mayor of New York City. Each had given the president lots of trouble.

Arriving at the office, Mr. Lincoln began work on the mass of material that, then as now, must be dealt with personally by the president of the United States. The pope, a king, a queen regnant, and the president never can take a vacation. These are 24-hour-a-day, 365-days-a-year jobs. Some of us have found that heads of corporations can't take vacations, either. Wherever they go, whatever they are doing, they literally are "on the job." Because of the almost incalculable workload imposed by the Civil War in addition to the normal heavy load of magisterial duties, the burden of government resting on Lincoln was greater than that of any of his fifteen predecessors.

It has been estimated that Lincoln personally signed an average of 100 documents every day. If this figure is even nearly accurate, his signing burden must have run to more than 30,000 a year.

On the day I have chosen to describe to you, Lincoln worked in his office alone that morning until about seven o'clock, when his secretaries, Nicolay, Hay, and William O. Stoddard, appeared and began dealing with the business of the new day, conferring with the president about documents, mail, appointments, and the duties of the moment. The next day, there was to be a Cabinet meeting, and they consulted their chief about the agenda.

As an interesting sidelight, Nicolay and Hay, in their correspondence with each other and in private conversations together, always referred affectionately to Lincoln as the "Ty-coon."

At eight o'clock, the president went to breakfast, which consisted of an egg, toast, and coffee. Lincoln was not a heavy eater. About noon, he ate a light luncheon. After each meal on the eighth, he returned promptly to his office.

The war situation on that February 8 was clearly favorable to the Union cause. Grant was holding and pressing Lee around Richmond in what was to prove to be the forepressure of the action that, the next April, would crush the Confederacy. There were skirmishes on February 8 at Ten Mile Run near Camp Finegan as the Florida expedition advanced from Jacksonville. Sherman's men skirmished at Coldwater Ferry, near Morton, and near Senatobia in Mississippi as part of the Meridian campaigning. Fighting also occurred at Barbourville, Kentucky; Ringgold, Georgia; near Maryville, Tennessee, and at Donaldsonville, Louisiana. There was no major engagement under way on the eighth.

On February 3, Lincoln had met at City Point, Virginia, with Alexander H. Stevens, vice-president of the Confederacy, and two other Southern leaders, J. A. Campbell and R. M. T. Hunter. They had been appointed by President Davis to confer with the federal government, looking toward a negotiated peace. The conference turned out to be futile, and on the eighth, which was the day of which I speak, the House of Representatives adopted a resolution asking the president to report on the conference. Lincoln went to work immediately with Secretary of State Seward to fulfill the request. The report, which is very complete with all the documents involved, was finished by February 10 and sent on that day by Seward to the House of Representatives, with a copy to the Senate.

In addition to this work, on the eighth, Lincoln settled a dispute between New Hampshire and Vermont about the number of draftees each should establish as a quota under a call for draft that was pending. Having made his decision, he wrote the governor of New Hampshire a carefully worded letter outlining it.

He also advised Congress by handwritten letter that while he had signed a joint resolution involving the right of

Congress to exclude from counting all electoral votes deemed by it to be illegal, his signature should not be regarded as an opinion on the practicability or legality of the resolution. Mr. Lincoln's care in outlining his position involved his own personal interest in the canvass by Congress of the votes of members of the Electoral College. His second inauguration was to be on the next fourth of March.

He asked Congress to decide on the propriety of Captain Henry S. Stellwagen, U.S.N., commander of the U.S. frigate *Constellation*, accepting a sword from Queen Victoria in token of gratitude for his services to the British brigantine *Mersey*. The British ship had stalled at sea because of a fault in the engines, Captain Stellwagen, sailing nearby on the *Constellation*, had stopped, boarded the *Mersey*, and effected complete repair. Victoria was grateful.

He considered the case of one James Taylor, who had been sentenced to be executed as a spy, and suspended the execution "until further orders." The boy later was pardoned.

He pardoned Private Michael Nash, 65th Ohio Volunteers, who was under sentence of death for desertion.

He promited 1st. Lt. George Monroe of the 54th Illinois Volunteers to a captaincy.

All during the day, telegrams of first importance received in the War Department telegraph room were forwarded to the White House, and those of urgency were referred to the president, who attended to them.

After a light dinner at six, at which no one but the family was present (hence no wine was served), the president returned to his office to complete the signing of documents. During the evening, as was the custom, his friends, Secretary Seward, Senator Browning, Marshal Lamon, Congressmen Washburne and Kelley, and Indian Commissioner Dole, dropped in to visit, and as he worked, the president relaxed, and as Hay described such evenings, "his wit and rich humor had free play and he was once more the Lincoln of the Eighth Circuit."

About eleven o'clock, the paper-signing task and other necessary work of the day completed, Lincoln walked over to the War Department, which was located near the White House. There, in the telegraph room, he read the news that had come over the wire and had been accumulated during the day. Thus, he knew where his armies were fighting or moving, how they were doing, and what was transpiring.

Let Benjamin Thomas, whom I have come to rate as probably the best and most reliable biographer of Lincoln, describe the scene in the telegraph room:

A visit to the War Department telegraph room was usually his last chore. The operators left copies of all military telegrams in a pile in a desk drawer for him, with the last dispatch on top. They noticed that as he read them he sat forward on the edge of his chair with one knee just touching the floor. When he had worked through the pile to the messages he had read before, he put all of them back and said, "Well, I have got down to the raisins."

The curiosity of the young operators got the best of them at last, and one of them asked the President what he meant by that remark. He told them that he had known a little girl back home who once gorged herself with a stupendous meal of soup, chicken, ham, potatoes and sundry other vegetables, ice cream and cake, and at last a hand full of raisins. Things began coming up; and after she had been busily engaged for some time, she looked up at her mother and said reassuringly; "I'm all right now. I've got down to the raisins."

Returning to the White House, Mr. Lincoln read a while and then went to bed to catch—if he could—about five or six hours of sleep. He seemed to require but about that much sleep each day. The telegraph operators noticed that he often carried a worn copy of *Macbeth* or *The Merry Wives of Windsor* under his arm when he made his last visit each day, to their office.

So ended February 8, 1865, for Abraham Lincoln.

No doubt you wonder why I have gone into detail to describe a single, relatively unimportant day in the life of Lincoln, the president. I do so because I think it gives us a clue to one of the attributes of his greatness: the simplicity and directness with which he went about his task of running the national government, winning the Civil War, and saving the Union.

Hay marveled, as he watched Lincoln day after day, that he could guide the machinery of government, manage the war, the draft, and foreign relations and plan a reconstruction of the Union all at once. Hay had never known anyone so wise, so gentle, and so strong. "He seemed called of God for his place" was Hay's opinion.

There is no sham, no pretense, no flamboyance, no pomposity, no deception, no deviation from his tenacious determination to achieve his one announced and all-absorbing goal: "I would save the Union."

His greatness was inherent within him, an endowment from the Almighty.

Mr. Lincoln's Private Secretaries

Officially, the White House payroll in the Lincoln administration listed one private secretary to the president. Actually, two young men acted in this capacity throughout Mr. Lincoln's tenure as chief magistrate, and the burden became so heavy at times that others were added to the staff by being "borrowed" from various departments of government.

John George Nicolay, a young Illinois newspaperman, who was an admirer and supporter of Mr. Lincoln in the years before and during 1858–1859, was drafted for secretarial duties by candidate Lincoln shortly after the nomination in 1860. During the campaign, the work became so heavy that Mr. Nicolay could not handle it alone, and he asked the president-elect if he could have young John Hay, another young Illinois writer and law student, to assist him, and Mr. Lincoln agreed.

So began the team of Nicolay and Hay, to whom history refers accurately as "Lincoln's secretaries." They were efficient, industrious, methodical, devoted, and loyal.

Almost up to the time for the president-elect to leave his home in Springfield and begin the journey to Washington, February 11, 1861, Nicolay had not settled the matter of Hay's joining him in Washington.

Realizing the extent of the demands in time and effort that would devolve on a "private secretary" to the president of the United States under the troublesome conditions that surrounded Mr. Lincoln's accession and feeling that he must have an assistant, a few days before departure, Nicolay asked Mr. Lincoln if he could take Hay, who had been so helpful in

Springfield, with him to Washington. There was acquiescence again, although Mr. Lincoln, as he nodded his head affirmatively, said, "We can't take everybody in Illinois." When the Lincoln special train pulled out of Springfield, Nicolay and Hay were aboard, and they were at the president's side throughout his administration.

John George Nicolay was born in the tiny village of Essinger, Bavaria, in 1832. In 1837, the family, including him and consisting of his father, John Jacob Nicolai (the spelling used until the trip to America): his mother, Helena Müller Nicolai; two brothers, John Jacob and John; and a sister, Catherine, came to the United States. The repetitious use of the name *John* among the siblings is interesting. The oldest son. Frederick Lewis Nicolai, had emigrated to America the year before.

In Germany, John Jacob had farmed a small tract of land and plied the cooper's trade, assisted by the older boys.

With their possessions on a two-wheel cart, they walked to Le Havre and took passage on a ship bound for New Orleans, then journeyed by packet up the Mississippi and Ohio rivers to Cincinnati, the destination they chose because of its large German population and because its schools were bilingual, teaching both in English and German.

In Cincinnati, John Jacob bought a lot, built a small house, enrolled his younger children in the public schools, and set himself up in the cooper's trade.

John George's mother died in Cincinnati and is buried here. Helen Nicolay (John G.'s daughter) tells, in her biography of her father, that after this sad event, her "grandfather became restless and moved his family successively into Indiana, Missouri and Illinois" where "the trek ended in the woods" in Pike County. John George became his father's "scribe and interpreter."

Clerking in a store later in his boyhood, John G. became interested in such newspapers as found their way into the frontier settlement, and, in 1848, at 16 years of age, he went to work as a "printer's devil" (as apprentices were known in those days) for the Pittsfield, Illinois, *Free Press*, a Whig newspaper. He worked his way up the ladder of journalism until, by 1854, he owned the paper.

Mr. Lincoln was one of the leading lawyers of Illinois, was active in politics, and was a relatively frequent visitor in Pittsfield. While there, he became acquainted with young Nicolay and took a liking to him and an interest in him. The young journalist became an active supporter of Mr. Lincoln.

Meanwhile, Nicolay had resolved to become a lawyer and acted promptly on his decision. He sold the *Free Press*, moved to Springfield and began the study of law under the preceptorship of a well-known attorney named Norman B. Coleman, at the same time becoming an employee of the secretary of state of Illinois. He also served the *Missouri Democrat*, the *Illinois Journal* and the *Chicago Tribune* as correspondent and, with all of these to keep him busy, settled down to an active business and social life in the thriving capital city of the state.

Naturally, a lawyer and politician of Mr. Lincoln's prominence saw a good deal of young Nicolay both in the office of the secretary of state and in his capacity as a newspaper correspondent. When the time came that nominee Lincoln needed a private secretary, he employed Nicolay, and the relationship lasted throughout the president's life.

John Hay, who was born and raised in Indiana, came to Pittsfield, Illinois, in 1851 to live with his uncle, John Milton Hay, while he was being tutored by a Pittsfield educator named John Thompson. The tutoring was to fit Hay for admission to Brown University. Nicolay and Hay formed a warm friendship. Hay went to Springfield to attend a college there and, in 1855, matriculated at Brown University in Providence, Rhode Island. He was sixteen years and eleven months old. He completed his course on June 10, 1858, having "made" Phi Beta Kappa, but did not stay for commencement, which was held in September.

Leaving Providence, the seat of Brown University, Hay returned to his parents' home in Warsaw, Illinois, with some thought of becoming a "poet and a man of letters."

However, by the spring of 1859, he had elected to become a lawyer and entered the office of his uncle, John Milton Hay, who then was practicing in Springfield, to "read law." On February 4, 1861, he was admitted to the bar.

But, before that event, he was to enlist as a secretary to

Abraham Lincoln and embark on a career such as few men have experienced.

Hay, was twenty-three years of age and Nicolay was twenty-nine comprised the permanent Lincoln secretariat.

Nicolay was on the White House payroll as private secretary to the president. There was no provision for a second secretary, but the need was great, for the demands on the president's time were greater than that of any of his predecessors, and with impending and later actual Civil War, Mr. Lincoln carried a burden that kept him busy day and night. The problem of a second secretary was solved by appointing Hay to a clerkship in the Department of the Interior and assigning him to special service in the White House.

Both secretaries lived in the White House and were on duty practically twenty-four hours a day. As work piled up, additional staff was provided from time to time and always by the device of having a clerk from one of the departments of the government assigned to the White House.

The first official act of the new president after he entered his office on March 4, 1861, was to sign the document appointing John G. Nicolay to be his private secretary.

Among those who from time to time helped Nicolay and Hay were William O. Stoddard, who was brought in from the Department of the Interior, Edward D. Neale, of Minnesota, and Charles H. Philbrick, of Illinois.

Both Nicolay and Hay entered the diplomatic service after Mr. Lincoln's death. Nicolay resigned his secretaryship on April 20, 1865, and went West to visit his family and friends. He married Miss Theresa Bates, with whom he had been in love since his days in Pittsfield. The wedding took place on June 15, 1865, and John Hay was his best man. The newlyweds then sailed for France, where Nicolay took up his duties as U.S. consul in Paris, where he served for four years.

Hay joined the Nicolays in Paris later that year, having been appointed secretary to the United States legation.

When Nicolay returned home, he engaged in journalistic pursuits and subsequently (in 1872) became marshal of the United States Supreme Court.

Hay's career was to take him into journalism and into the state department as assistant secretary. Subsequently, he served as Ambassador to the Court of St. James's and was secretary of state under Presidents McKinley and Theodore Roosevelt.

Nicolay and Hay were asked by President Lincoln's son, Robert Todd Lincoln, to take charge of his father's papers, to edit and publish them, and to be the president's official biographers, doing this work jointly. This monumental task occupied much of their time for some twenty years and resulted in two carefully researched and well-edited and written works: *Abraham Lincoln: Complete Works*, an eleven-volume work, and *Abraham Lincoln: A History*, published by *Century* magazine in serial form beginning in 1886 and in 10 volumes in 1890.

Nicolay wrote voluminously about Mr. Lincoln in addition to his editorial work on the *Complete Works* and his coauthorship of the biography. Best known are his one-volume condensation *Life of Lincoln* and his *Outbreak of Rebellion*. In addition, he wrote many contributions to magazines in the latter part of the nineteenth century.

Mr. Nicolay died September 26, 1901.

Mr. Hay died July 1, 1905.

Lincoln Founds Washington Police Force

Early in his administration, President Lincoln established the Metropolitan Police Department of the city of Washington.

A captain and fifteen patrolmen constituted the "Night Watch," which patrolled at night and was the only police activity in the capital city when Mr. Lincoln took office as president. The group of watchmen was unequal to coping with the task of keeping the peace as the Civil War approached reality in the fall of 1860 and the winter of 1861. "Hordes of unsavory characters descended upon the Federal City—crooks, gamblers, prostitutes, pickpockets and thugs," writes George R. Wilson of the Metropolitan Police Department in a recent article in the *F.B.I. Enforcement Bulletin.*

One observer is quoted as saying that a "tent and shack city" not far from the army encampment, which stretched for five miles along the Maryland shore of the Potomac River, was "the longest and busiest brothel in the world."

The seriousness of the crime problem and the necessity for creating a police force adequate to cope with it was brought to the attention of President Lincoln, and he recommended to Congress that legislation be enacted creating a regular full-time police force for the District.

Congress acted affirmatively on his recommendation, and the act creating the Metropolitan Police Department became law on August 6, 1861.

The president then instructed Zenas C. Robbins, whom he had appointed to the board of Metropolitan Police commissioners, to go to New York City and study the New York police system, which had been modeled on the London plan, and that was done.

Mr. Robbins's report recommended a metropolitan-type police organization of the kind in operation in New York. It was adopted by the Washington commissioners, and the new force was organized promptly. Melvin B. Webb was appointed superintendent, and the first personnel roll included, under command of the superintendent, 10 sergeants and 150 patrolmen. It immediately began the task of policing the nation's capital and attempting to enforce the laws twenty-four hours a day, 365 days a year.

According to the requirements established by the board of commissioners, Mr. Webb took great care in selecting men of "good repute, sound mind and good health," all of whom were between twenty-five and forty-five years of age. The superintendent's salary was $1,500 a year. Sergeants were paid $600 annually and patrolmen $480. The men were divided into two shifts working twelve hours each. Each furnished his own handgun. As of last report, the personnel now (1977) numbers 4,550 men and women, and the annual budget is $91 million.

And crime is more rampant in Washington than it was in 1861.

Two Cincinnatians—Lincoln's
Greatest Personnel Problem

The pressures for patronage that beset Mr. Lincoln from the moment of his election through the days before and after inauguration in 1860 and through 1861 and 1862, tapering off somewhat thereafter, were heavier than those experienced by any of his predecessors because (1) Mr. Lincoln was the first president elected by a newly formed party, the Republican party, and (2) he faced a large demand for commissions in the huge army formed to win the Civil War.

Prior to 1860, all presidents except Washington had been elected under one of the following political designations: Federalist, Democratic-Republican (as the Democratic party was first called), Democrat, or Whig.

George Washington, particularly, was above party, although historians credit him to the Federalists. He received all of the electoral votes cast in the first two presidential elections. John Adams (Federalist) and Thomas Jefferson (Democratic-Republican) staged the first political campaign for the presidency in 1796. Adams won with seventy-one electoral votes to sixty-eight for Jefferson.

One of the most interesting contests was that in the year 1800 when two Democratic-Republicans, Jefferson and Aaron Burr, ran against each other and the vote in the Electoral College was tied at seventy-three. The House of Representatives broke the tie by electing Jefferson.

In 1860, however, there was a wide swing in votes to the new Republican party, which drew support from both Whigs and Democrats. (Lincoln had been a member of the Whig party and was termed an "Old Whig.") He had to face massive desire for federal jobs from those who had formed the new party, both Whigs and Democrats.

But of all the myriad personnel problems, political and military, that beset and harassed Mr. Lincoln, Ohio and, to be specific, Cincinnati presented the two most vexatious and most difficult. These were Gen. George Brinton McClellan and Secretary of the Treasury Salmon P. Chase.

While charging Ohio with these two most difficult of Lincoln's people, it should be interpolated here that more than counterbalancing the worries caused by McClellan and Chase, Ohio also gave Lincoln, Grant, and Sherman and Sheridan and Stanton, to name just a few, who, by their war-winning achievements, balanced the good heavily on the credit side of Ohio's contributions in leadership.

A West Point graduate in the class of 1846, finishing second in a class of fifty-nine, McClellan served as an engineer subaltern in the war with Mexico and was cited for gallantry and for ability in constructing roads and bridges. He won brevets of first lieutenant and captain. After the war, he taught at West Point and thereafter was sent to the Crimea as an observer of the British-French war with Russia. He came home a captain but soon resigned his commission to put his engineering education to work as president of the eastern division of the Ohio and Mississippi Railroad (forerunner of the Illinois Central) and was earning what then was the truly magnificent salary of $10,000 per year. His headquarters was in Cincinnati, and he maintained his residence in that city.

With the outbreak of war, the governors of Ohio and Pennsylvania both sought McClellan, then thirty-five years of age, to command the troops being recruited and trained in their states. Gov. Andrew G. Curtin of Pennsylvania sent for him to come to Harrisburg to discuss the matter.

Bruce Catton, in his splendid *Mr. Lincoln's Army** tells of McClellan's starting for Harrisburg and stopping off in Columbus, where he called on Ohio's governor, William Dennison. Dennison immediately told him of his own problems. He was recruiting 10,000 Ohio men, who had to be converted into soldiers, uniformed, housed, armed, trained, and transported to the war zone, wherever the U.S. Army wanted them

*Quoted with permission of Mr. Catton and Mr. Williams.

and where they would become part of that army. He offered McClellan a commission as a major general of volunteers and Captain McClellan accepted. As General McClellan, he went to work immediately.

Catton writes:

It is interesting to speculate about the difference there would have been in McClellan's career had he gone on to Harrisburg and taken command of the Pennsylvania troops instead of staying in Ohio. Fame would have come much more slowly, and he would have had a chance to adjust himself to it. Pennsylvania sent a solid division down to Washington shortly after Bull Run. It was the division McClellan would have commanded had he gone to Harrisburg; it contained good men and had some first-class officers, and it was just the right organization to build a solid reputation for its commanding general—it brought George C. Meade up to the command of the Army of the Potomac in 1863, after giving him plenty of time to prove himself and to find himself in battle. What would McClellan's luck have been with that division? No immediate limelight, comparative obscurity during the army's early days—what would have become of him, anyway?

(Another might-have-been: there came to McClellan's Ohio headquarters one day that spring a former infantry captain, somewhat seedy, presenting himself as a one-time acquaintance of the general looking for work; name of U.S. Grant. Was there a place for him, perhaps, on McClellan's staff? The general was away that day, and Grant was told to come back later. Instead of coming back Grant went west and finally wangled command of a regiment of Illinois volunteers. McClellan would have given him a staff job if he had seen him. What, one wonders, would Grant's future have been in that case?)

By the latter days of May 1861, the Ohio volunteers had been whipped into some kind of military shape and mustered into U.S. service.

By this time, also, the Confederates had sent troops into the western part of Virginia where the population was strongly pro-Union. The Southerners were cutting the main rail line from Washington to Cincinnati, the Baltimore and Ohio Railroad, and the federal government ordered McClellan and his Ohio troops into the area to drive out the "Rebs" and to regain and repair the railroad. Sixteen regiments from

Ohio, nine from Indiana, and two composed of Union-minded Virginians from the Parkersburg and Wheeling areas constituted McClellan's army.

McClellan moved into the mountains and routed the Confederates. Everything west of the Allegheny Mountains was then cleared of Confederate troops, and the Baltimore and Ohio Railroad resumed service vitally needed for the war effort. Subsequently, the state of West Virginia was erected in this territory and was admitted to the Union.

McClellan was the hero of the hour; he was ordered to Washington and given command of the Army. And it went to his head.

After a few months of being pampered by Congress and the executive, his egotism took control of his personality, revealing a huge inferiority complex. He became arrogant, domineering, rude, insulting, defiant, and used every device he could conjure to avoid battle contact with the Confederacy.

"Who would have thought, when we were married," he wrote to his wife, Ellen Mary Marcy McClellan, "that I would so soon be called upon to save my country?"

In another letter to Mrs. McClellan, he wrote that he was getting used to the comment "Why, how young you look and yet an old soldier!" "All tell me," one letter read, "that I am held responsible for the fate of the nation, and that all its resources shall be placed at my disposal. It is an immense task that I have on my hands, but I believe I can accomplish it."

Again, he wrote, "The people call upon me to save the country. I must save it, and cannot respect anything that is in the way." And,

I receive letter after letter, have conversation after conversation, calling on me to save the nation, alluding to the presidency, dictatorship, etc. As I hope to be united with you one day in Heaven, I have no such aspiration. I would cheerfully take the dictatorship and agree to lay down my life when the country is saved. I am not spoiled by my unexpected new position.

When he wrote this, he had been in Washington not quite two weeks and back in the army but a short four months.

What a pity that Mr. Lincoln could not have referred the "little Napoleon" to a psychiatrist. He might have been straightened out and have overcome his fears.

Subsequently, McClellan replaced General Winfield Scott, a hero of the Mexican War, who retired as chief of staff because of age and infirmities. With that assignment, McClellan occupied the center of the state of war in the East. His troops idolized him, and he trained them well, but he could not be motivated to fight.

Finally, President Lincoln brought enough pressure by direct order to force him to invade Virginia. Union troops got within five miles of Richmond but were driven out by Lee, and the invasion was a costly failure. McClellan insisted throughout that he was outnumbered, but he was not. Accurate intelligence, available in Washington, revealed that his army greatly exceeded the Confederate forces. He insisted on vastly overestimating the Confederate forces and refused to resume the offensive until given reinforcements that the then general-in-chief, General Halleck, refused to provide, knowing that McClellan had sufficient men under his command to succeed. With the failure of that campaign, McClellan was ordered to bring his army back to Washington and was relieved of command.

He was later restored to command and given the job of reorganizing the Army of the Potomac, which he did well. The battle of Antietam followed, in 1863, and McClellan had an opportunity to destroy Lee's army, but again he failed. He refused to move in time, although Lincoln ordered him so to do. Lincoln then again removed him from command, and his active career as a soldier was over.

T. Harry Williams, author of *Lincoln and His Generals**, writes:

McClellan is the problem child of the Civil War. People reacted to him in violent extremes but rarely in terms of realistic evaluation. His contemporaries revered or reviled him, and historians have defended or attacked him. There was a duality in his character that made him at once honest and deceitful, simple and cunning, modest

*(From *Lincoln and His Generals*, by T. Harry Williams. Copyright 1952 by Alfred A. Knopf, Inc. Reprinted by permission of the publisher.

and arrogant, attractive and distasteful. Some people saw one McClellan; some, the other. Lincoln saw both, and labored patiently to bring the good McClellan uppermost. The job was too difficult even for his talents of human management.

McClellan's dilatory tactics resulted in his loyalty being questioned, and his ambition to run for president became the overweening objective of his life.

McClellan was nominated by the Democratic party as its candidate for president in 1864.

An entry in John Hay's diary for Sunday, September 25, 1864, is very revealing. In it, he quotes the president about McClellan. Hay wrote:

September 25, Sunday. 1864. Yesterday Nicolay, who has been several days in New York, telegraphed to the President that Thurlow Weed had gone to Canada and asking if he, N., had better return. I answered he had better amuse himself there for a day or two. This morning a letter came in the same sense. The President, when I showed it to him, said, "I think I know where Mr W. has gone. I think he has gone to Vermont, not Canada. I will tell you what he is trying to do. I have not as yet told anybody.

"Sometime ago the Governor of Vermont came to see me 'on business of importance,' he said. I fixed an hour & he came. His name is Smith. He is, though you wouldn't think it, a cousin of Baldy Smith. Baldy is large, blond, florid. The Governor is a little dark phystey sort of man. This is the story he told me, giving General Baldy Smith as his authority.

"When General McClellan was here at Washington, Baldy Smith was very intimate with him. They had been together at West Point & friends. McClellan had asked for promotion for Baldy from the President & got it. They were close and confidential friends. When they went down to the Peninsula their same intimate relations continued, the General talking freely with Smith about all his plans and prospects: until one day Fernando Wood & one other politician from New York appeared in camp & passed some days with McClellan. From the day that this took place, Smith saw, or thought he saw, that McClellan was treating him with unusual coolness & reserve. After a little while he mentioned this to McC. who after some talk told Baldy he had something to show him. He told him that these people who had recently visited him, had been urging him to stand as an opposition candidate for President: that he had thought the thing over, and had concluded to accept their

59

propositions & had written them a letter (which he had not yet sent) giving his idea of the proper way of conducting the war, so as to conciliate and impress the people of the South with the idea that our armies were intended merely to execute the laws and protect their property, &c., & pledging himself to conduct the war in that inefficient conciliatory style. This letter he read to Baldy, who after the reading was finished said earnestly, 'General, do you not see that looks like treason: & that it will ruin you and all of us?' After some further talk the General destroyed the letter in Baldy's presence, and thanked him heartily for his frank & friendly counsel. After this he was again taken into the intimate confidence of McClellan. Immediately after the Battle of Antietam Wood & his familiars came again & saw the General, & again Baldy saw an immediate estrangement on the part of McClellan. He seemed to be anxious to get his intimate friends out of the way and to avoid opportunities of private conversation with them. Baldy, he particularly kept employed on reconnoissances and such work. One night Smith was returning from some duty he had been performing & seeing a light in McClellan's tent he went in to report. Several persons were there. He reported & was about to withdraw when the General requested him to remain. After everyone was gone he told him those men had been there again and had renewed their proposition about the Presidency—that this time he had agreed to their proposition and had written them a letter acceding to their terms and pledging himself to carry on the war in the sense already indicated. This letter he read then and there to Baldy Smith.

"Immediately thereafter Baldy Smith applied to be transferred from that army.

"At very nearly the same time other prominent men asked the same, Franklin, Burnside and others.

"Now that letter must be in the possession of Fernando Wood, and it will not be impossible to get it. Mr Weed has, I think, gone to Vermont to see the Smiths about it."

I was very much surprised at the story & expressed my surprise. I said I had always thought that McClellan's fault was a constitutional weakness and timidity which prevented him from active and timely exertion, instead of any such deep-laid scheme of treachery & ambition.

The President replied, "After the battle of Antietam, I went up to the field to try to get him to move & came back thinking he would move at once. But when I got home he began to argue why he ought not to move. I peremptorily ordered him to advance. It was 19 days before he put a man over the river. It was 9 days longer before he got his army across and then he stopped again, delaying on the little pretexts of wanting this and that. I began to fear he was playing false—that he did not want to hurt the enemy. I saw how he could intercept the enemy on the way to Richmond. I determined to make that the test. If he let them get away I would remove him. He did so & I relieved him.

"I dismissed Major Key for his silly treasonable talk because I feared it was staff talk & I wanted an example.

"The letter of Buell furnishes another evidence in support of that theory. And the story you have heard Neill tell about Seymour's first visit to McClellan all tallies with this story."

Thus did Lincoln deal with McClellan, one of his worst personnel problems.

When the election returns were in, McClellan had carried only New Jersey, Delaware, and Kentucky, with twenty-one electoral votes. Lincoln had carried all the rest, with 212 electoral votes. Lincoln lived immortal in history. McClellan is but a footnote near oblivion.

Cincinnati's second contribution to Mr. Lincoln's vexations was Salmon P. Chase, a politically active and very successful lawyer whom the president appointed secretary of the Treasury.

Like McClellan, Chase had great ability and, also like McClellan, an overweening ambition and a consuming egotism. The result was a constant stirring to do things his way instead of Lincoln's, a continual criticism of Lincoln, to whom Chase believed himself to be superior in ability and social standing, and a never-ending politicking to defeat Lincoln for nomination for a second term and to become the candidate himself.

Lincoln exhibited the same patient endeavor to get the maximum results from Chase's ability that he exercised toward McClellan and put up with the Chase intransigence for nearly four years before terminating his services as secretary of the Treasury.

Chase was a native of New Hampshire, where he was born in 1808. His father died in 1817, and young Salmon was brought to Ohio, where he made his home with an uncle, Philander Chase, bishop of the Protestant Episcopal Church.

Salmon's Uncle Philander was an industrious and strong-minded churchman. He began his ministerial career as a missionary priest who came to Ohio to organize and develop Episcopal churches. He located in Worthington, Ohio, where he organized St. John's Episcopal Church, the first of that denomination in this state. Christ Church, Cincinnati; Trinity, Columbus; All Saints, Portsmouth; St. Paul's, Chillicothe, and many others owe their existence to Bishop Chase. He was elected bishop in 1819, the first ordinary to serve the newly created Ohio diocese.

Bishop Chase founded two colleges: Kenyon, in Ohio, and Jubilee, in Illinois.

Leaving Ohio in 1831, he went to Illinois, where he repeated his success in organizing Episcopal parishes and where he became bishop of the diocese of Illinois in 1835.

In 1843, Chase became presiding bishop of the Protestant Episcopal Church in the United States, a post he held until his death in 1852.

It was under the foster fatherhood of this aggressive churchman that Salmon Chase grew to manhood.

After being graduated from Dartmouth College in 1826, Salmon Chase went to Washington; he studied law there under the preceptorship of William Wirt, attorney general of the United States and was admitted to practice in 1829. A year later, he moved to Cincinnati and opened a law office.

Chase developed a good practice rapidly and became active in the civic and business life of the community. He gained statewide fame for a number of cases in which he represented fugitive slaves.

In 1849, Chase was elected to the U.S. Senate. At that time, he classified himself as an independent Democrat. By 1855, however, he had become affiliated with the then newly forming Republican party and was the first Republican to be elected to the office of governor in Ohio. He served in the governorship until 1859, at which time he began and waged an active campaign for the Republican nomination for president in 1860. However, it was not to be. Mr. Lincoln won the nomination, and Chase was angered when most of Ohio's delegates left his support and voted for Lincoln, giving the Illinoisan the votes that "put him over" for the nomination.

Immediately after the election in 1860, Chase, aided by his politically ambitious, active, and beautiful daughter, Kate, began to line up support for appointment to the Cabinet, and their goal was the top office, that of secretary of state. They hoped in vain, of course, for Lincoln's choice for that post from the beginning was William H. Seward of New York.

On December 31, 1860, Lincoln sent Chase a telegram asking him to come to Springfield for a conference, and Chase went there on January 3, 1861.

Lincoln was very frank with Chase. He knew that the Ohioan wanted to be secretary of state, so he told him, at the outset of the conversation, according to what Chase told his daughter, that he had chosen Seward for secretary of state and that if Seward had declined, he would have offered the position to Chase. Seward, having accepted, the president-elect asked Chase to become secretary of the Treasury, an office that then, as now, is considered second in ranking in the cabinet.

As Kate Sprague's biographer, Ishbel Ross, tells it, Chase, chagrined at the offer of second place, "told Lincoln coldly that he was 'not prepared to say that he would accept the place if offered,' and he desired to ask the advice of his friends."

"In actual fact," biographer Ross continues, "he wanted to talk it over with Kate and to consult Sumner and his newspaper friends in Park Row."

Although Kate was resentful at what she thought was shabby treatment on top of Chase's defeat for the nomination, his and her ambition prevailed when they realized that Treasury was better than nothing, and he took the appointment.

One comment of the *Encyclopaedia Britannica* on Chase's services as secretary of the Treasury is revealing: "Perhaps Chase's chief defeat as a statesman was his insatiable desire for supreme office."

Throughout his services as head of Treasury, while struggling with the problems of financing the government during the war, he was constantly building political fences in an effort to win the nomination in 1864 over Lincoln. He feuded with Seward and other members of the cabinet and was in continual conspiracy for his own advancement. Despite all of this, Lincoln put up with him and supported him in his services as secretary of the Treasury because of his success in the difficult task of financing the war and in founding, in 1863, the national banking system of the United States.

In 1864, however, the feuding heated up to a point when, on a June day, a sulking and petulant Chase submitted his resignation, expecting the president to reject it, as he had done when the hypocritical resignation threat was tried before. But Lincoln gave him the shock of his life: he accepted it, and Chase walked out of the president's office a stunned and angry private citizen.

Lincoln, of course, was renominated and reelected handily.

On December 6, 1864, Chief Justice Roger Taney died, and Lincoln, who never held a grudge, believing Chase's ability as a lawyer qualified him for the job, appointed Chase chief justice of the United States.

Chases passion for the presidency never died down, however; he ran for the Democratic nomination in 1872 but was unsuccessful. He died in New York City in 1873.

The building that housed Chase's law office is still standing at Third and Main streets in Cincinnati, although the first floor is occupied by a cocktail lounge which once was called, of all things, "The Funeral Parlor."

At the University of Northern Kentucky, the College of Law is called the Chase College.

But the most famous memorial to Chase is a tribute to his ability as a financier of the republic during the Civil War and the founding of the national banking system. Because of these achievements, the great Chase Manhattan Bank, N.A., of New York City was named in his honor, as is the Chase National Life Insurance Company of Springfield, Missouri.

Lincoln and the Lady Who
Would Be a Chaplain

In these days of all the furor over whether women should be ordained as "clergymen," it is interesting to know that President Lincoln had to deal with the question during the Civil War.

There is one instance in which the problem of whether women could be chaplains in the army was put squarely up to President Lincoln by a lady from Wisconsin who had gotten herself elected chaplain of a Wisconsin regiment.

The lady was Mrs. Ella E. Gibson Hobart, an ordained minister of a church known as the Religio-Philosophical Society of St. Charles, Illinois.

Not only did Mrs. Hobart claim that her election as chaplain was unanimous, but also the colonel of the regiment confirmed the fact.

The War Department took a dim view of her claim. A woman clergyman? A woman chaplain working in the camps and in the battle lines? She must be out of her tree!

But the lady was persistent. She went to Washington and took her plea to the commander-in-chief.

One would have enjoyed being a witness at the interview. Here was the harassed war president, sympathetic to all who sought his help, taking time out to listen to an emotionally distraught woman who had run into the War Department's bureaucracy head-on, had been rejected, and then had rushed to the Mr. Lincoln for help.

What did she get? A note from the president to the secretary of war that is a masterpiece of sidestepping. The note reads:

November 10, 1864

This lady would be appointed Chaplain of the First Wisconsin Heavy Artillery, only that she is a woman. The President has not legally anything to do with the question, but he has no objection to her appointment.

A. Lincoln

So, armed with a note from the president to the secretary of War, the Reverend Mrs. Hobart trotted over to the War Department. The record does not indicate whether Secretary Stanton took the trouble to see her personally, but it does reveal what happened.

Secretary Stanton knew that the carefully written note was not only not an order from the commander-in-chief but was so written as to say, in between the lines, "Edwin, my friend, this is your hot potato—you handle it any way you wish, but I have 'no objection to her appointment.' "

So Mr. Stanton did just what the president and everybody involved would have done in 1864: he "declined to recognize the mustering on account of her sex, not wishing to establish a precedent."

But no one could accuse the president of being opposed to women preachers, priests, rabbis, or chaplains because he said in writing that he had "no objection to her appointment."

One wonders why in the present disputation over the ordination of women, Lincoln has not been quoted as "favoring" their ordination? The record would reply: he didn't favor it, but he had no objection to it!

Gettysburg Revisited

President Lincoln did not write the Gettysburg Address on a torn piece of borrowed brown wrapping paper while traveling by train to the ceremony of dedication, although Mary Raymond Shipman Andrews wrote that he did in her emotional little book *The Perfect Tribute*. Her perpetuation of that legend made her and her publishers a good deal of money and established the myth as fact in the minds of generations of people all over the world.

Quite the contrary, the Gettysburg Address was days in preparation in the president's mind, was written before he left Washington on the day before the ceremony to go to Gettysburg, and was revised subsequent to delivery.

There are five surviving copies of the address in Lincoln's handwriting. Two of these have come down to us from the papers of the president's private secretaries, John G. Nicolay and John Hay. They were given to the Library of Congress in 1916 by Hay's children and are known as "First Draft" or "Nicolay Copy," and "Second Draft" or "Hay Copy."

The first page of the "First Draft" is written on ruled stationery, approximately 7½ inches × 9 inches in measurement and headed "Executive Mansion, Washington —————— 186——." The date is left blank. The last sentence on this page reads, "It is rather for us, the living, to stand here." The words "to stand here" are crossed out and the words "we here be dedicated" written in. While the rest of the text is written in ink, the revision is in pencil, and since it does not fit the rest of the sentence grammatically, it would seem to have been a hastily written note to remind the president of a change that he intended to make and that, subsequently, he made.

The second page is on ruled paper about 7¾ inches wide and 13½ inches long that bears no identifying heading. The publisher of my photocopy says the pages were slightly reduced in reproduction. The text is written in ink and begins with the syllable "ted," apparently completing the word "dedicated." It appears to have had penciled notes at the top that have been erased and are not legible. Neither page is numbered.

The "First Draft" was written in Washington before November 18 (the day before the address was delivered), a fact that disproves the brown-paper-on-the-train tale.

The "First Draft" is in essence the address as Lincoln delivered it on November 19, 1863, but the best evidence I have found indicates that he did not read the address but delivered it from memory, holding a copy to refresh his mind if he faltered. It was in delivering the address that he probably interpolated the words "here to the unfinished work which they have, thus far, so nobly carried on," which are not in the "First Draft," and the most respected authorities believe that it was while he was speaking that he first added the words "under God."

The "Second Draft" or "Hay Copy" contains important modification and apparently was written at the executive mansion shortly after the dedication ceremonies. It is in ink on unruled paper. The photocopy that I have shows the first page to be about 7½ inches wide and 9 inches long. The second page is shown as about 7½ inches wide and 12½ inches long. However, again the publisher says, "The facsimile is slightly reduced," so I cannot be certain of the exact dimensions of the pages.

The Library of Congress comments as follows on the "Second Draft":

There is little evidence to support claims that this was the reading copy or that it was made in Gettysburg on the morning of November 19. Rather, the evidence suggests that it is more likely a copy made shortly after Lincoln's return to Washington. Possibly Lincoln made this copy for David Wills (his host in Gettysburg) in compliance with his request for 'the original manuscript' but gave it instead to John Hay.

In the "First Draft," Lincoln wrote of "a final resting place for those who died here" and changed it in the "Second" to "for those who here gave their lives." In the "First Draft," he wrote, "This we may, in all propriety do"; in the "Second," "It is altogether fitting and proper that we should do this."

In the "First Draft," he says, "the nation shall have a new birth of freedom"; in the "Second," it is "this" nation. In the "First," it is "government of the people"; in the "Second," it is "this government of the people." The "Second Draft" also differs from the "First" in that it contains the words "It is for us, the living, rather, to be dedicated here to the unfinished work which they have, thus far, so nobly carried on."

This idea is revised in a much more beautiful and eloquent way in what will be referred to later as the "Everett Copy" in which Mr. Lincoln has changed it to read, "It is for us, the living, rather, to be dedicated here to the unfinished work which they who fought here have thus far so nobly advanced."

In the fourth revision, the "Bancroft Copy," with which we will be dealing later in this writing, he uses the same sentence as in the "Everett Copy," and he keeps the same language in the fifth and apparently last revision, known as the "Bliss Copy."

A comparison of the first two drafts indicates that as Mr. Lincoln made the "Second Draft," he improved it, made it more forceful, and polished it considerably, but the essential thought was not changed.

Newspaper versions of the address, printed from transcribed shorthand notes made as it was delivered, carry the words "under God," which substantiate the belief that Mr. Lincoln spoke those words in delivering it, although they are not in the "First Draft."

Edward Everett, who had made the principal address at the Gettysburg ceremonies, had, on the next day, written to the president: "I should be glad if I could flatter myself that I came as near to the central idea of the occasion in two hours as you did in two minutes." Dr. Everett asked for a copy, and Mr. Lincoln made one for him. In the "Everett Copy," the phrase "under God" appears for the first time in Lincoln's handwriting. It is interesting that Lincoln wrote to Everett: "In our respective parts yesterday you could not have been excused to make a short address, nor I a long one. I am pleased to know that, in your judgment, the little I did say was not a failure."

The fourth copy made by Mr. Lincoln is known as the "Bancroft Copy," for it was made at the request of historian George Bancroft for his stepson and was to be one of a series of lithographed facsimiles to be sold to raise money for the benefit of the Baltimore Sanitary Fair, held by the commission that served the soldiers of the Union Army much as the Red Cross does today.

Aside from minor changes in punctuation, the only difference between the "Bancroft Copy" and the "Everett Copy" is the use of "on" instead of "upon" in the first sentence, which, in the "Bancroft Copy," reads: "Four score and seven years ago our fathers brought forth on this continent a new nation," etc. One would suspect that this was an error made in the haste of copying, for it is the only copy Mr. Lincoln wrote wherein he did not use "upon."

The fifth copy that Mr. Lincoln wrote is known as the "Bliss Copy," and this last holograph was written by the president in response to a request by John P. Kennedy, editor of the volume of facsimiles that was being prepared for the fair at Baltimore. Mr. Kennedy returned the "Bancroft Copy," asking the president to write another one for publication by the Sanitary Commission, one that would meet certain standards as to size of paper and margins and that would be given a heading and would bear the president's signature. The president's secretary asked Mr. Kennedy to supply the paper he wished used so that there would be no question as to its size being correct, and this was done by a Col. Alexander Bliss. Mr. Lincoln then wrote the requested copy and sent it, together with the "Bancroft Copy," to Bliss, whose name it has borne in subsequent years as an identification.

The Library of Congress publication on the address says of the "Bliss Copy":

Since it represents Lincoln's last-known revision, it has become accepted as the standard text, although it differs from the Bancroft copy, aside from punctuation, only in the omission of "here" in the phrase "they here gave." The Bliss copy is the only one dated and signed by President Lincoln.

Hence, the consensus of authorities is that it is the one most nearly like what Lincoln said at Gettysburg, certainly what he intended to say.

"The original," the Library goes on to relate, "remained with Col. Bliss and his family until 1949, when it was sold at an auction in New York City." The purchaser was a former ambassador to the United States from Cuba, Sr. Oscar B. Cintas of Havana. "By his will, the copy became the property of the people of this country, and, at his stipulation, it is now installed in the Lincoln Room in the White House."

In all literature, so far as I know, no more profound or beautifully composed memorial, civic, patriotic, or philosophic address can be found. It has been compared to the Sermon on the Mount in quality and to the 90th Psalm in depth of spirituality.

As the Lincoln scholar Benjamin Thomas wrote: "In 268 well-chosen words he gave America a chart and compass for the years ahead."

As I contemplate our own times, I believe that the Gettysburg Address becomes even more significant and important than Thomas's appraisal. It seems to me a solemn call to duty, sounding clearly over more than a century later to every devotee of liberty in the world.

Following is the text of the "Bliss Copy:"

Four score and seven years ago our fathers brought forth on this continent, a new nation, conceived in Liberty, and dedicated to the proposition that all men are created equal.

Now we are engaged in a great civil war, testing whether that nation, or any nation so conceived and so dedicated, can long endure. We are met on a great battle field of that war. We have come to dedicate a portion of that field, as a final resting place for those

71

who here gave their lives that that nation might live. It is altogether fitting and proper that we should do this.

But, in a larger sense, we can not dedicate—we can not consecrate—we can not hallow—this ground. The brave men, living and dead, who struggled here, have consecrated it, far above our poor power to add or detract. The world will little note, nor long remember what we say here, but it can never forget what they did here. It is for us the living, rather, to be dedicated here to the unfinished work which they who fought here have thus far so nobly advanced. It is rather for us to be here dedicated to the great task remaining before us—that from these honored dead we take increased devotion to that cause for which they gave the last full measure of devotion—that we here highly resolve that these dead shall not nave died in vain—that this nation, under God, shall have a new birth of freedom—and that government of the people, by the people, for the people, shall not perish from the earth.

In these days of concern for the fate of freedom in America, indeed throughout the free world, where can free men learn more of the awesome challenge they face than from these 268 simple, forthright words of Abraham Lincoln? What more is there for us to embrace as our sublime duty than to highly resolve that the hallowed, sacrificial dead who have laid down their lives for freedom on a multitude of battlefields throughout the world "shall not have died in vain"; "that this nation," which must survive as free if freedom is to survive in the world, "under God shall have a new birth of freedom" and that "government of the people, by the people, for the people shall not perish from the earth"?

If a merciful God grants our prayers and if we rally those who abhore tyranny, we can restore liberty here in America, and freedom may yet illumine even the darkest corner of earth to the glory of God's humblest creature, wherever he may be.

Address delivered at the dedication of the
Cemetery at Gettysburg.

Four score and seven years ago our fathers
brought forth on this continent, a new nation, conceived in Liberty, and dedicated
to the proposition that all men are created equal.

Now we are engaged in a great civil war,
testing whether that nation, or any nation
so conceived and so dedicated, can long
endure. We are met on a great battle-field
of that war. We have come to dedicate a
portion of that field, as a final resting
place for those who here gave their lives,
that that nation might live. It is altogether fitting and proper that we should
do this.

But in a larger sense, we can not dedicate— we can not consecrate— we can not hallow— this ground. The brave men, living and dead, who struggled here, have consecrated it, far above our poor power to add or detract. The world will little note, nor long remember what we say here, but it can never forget what they did here. It is for us the living, rather, to be dedicated here to the unfinished work which they who fought here have thus far so nobly advanced. It is rather for us to be here dedicated to the great task remaining before us— that from these honored dead we take increased devotion to that cause for which they gave the last full measure of devotion— that we here highly resolve that these dead shall not have died in vain— that this nation, under God, shall have a new birth of freedom— and that government of the people,

by the people, for the people, shall not per-
ish from the earth.

Abraham Lincoln

November 19, 1863.

This is a photograph of the Gettysburg address in Mr. Lincoln's handwriting written for Col. Alexander Bliss. The original is in the Lincoln room in the White House. The author gratefully acknowledges permission to publish this photograph granted by Miss Betty C. Monkman, Registrar of the Curator of the White House, Mr. Clement Conger. It is from the "White House Collection."

Spending Election Day, 1864,
With President Lincoln

The first Tuesday after the first Monday in November in the year 1864 fell on the eighth, which resulted in the presidential election that year coming as late in the month as ever it can.

It was a tense time. Could a republic *have* an election in time of civil war? Under such circumstances of dissension and division, could it survive a political campaign? These questions had been troubling the leaders of the country for months, and November eighth brought the "moment of truth."

On the night after the election, addressing a huge crowd with banners, lanterns, and transparencies that had marched to the White House to cheer the president, Mr. Lincoln expressed his thoughts about an election in time of civil war. Standing in an open window with his intimate friend Noah Brooks, a newspaper reporter holding a candle to light his manuscript, the president remarked that "the country had been sorely tested by days of hate, mistrust and bitterness."

"If the loyal people, united were put to the utmost of their strength by the rebellion, must they not fail when *divided* and practically paralyzed by a political war among themselves?" he asked.

But the election was a necessity. We cannot have free government without elections; and if the rebellion could force us to forego or postpone a national election it might fairly claim to have already conquered and ruined us . . . But the election along with its incidental and undesirable strife, has done us good, too. It has demonstrated that a people's government can sustain a national election in the midst of a great civil war. Until now it has not been known to the world that this was a possibility.

On election day, the White House was like the eye of a hurricane, "still and almost deserted." All who could do so had gone home to vote, for this was in the days before absentee voting by mail. Either you showed up at your regular voting place and cast your ballot, or you couldn't vote. The only exception was that a few states allowed their soldiers to vote in the field of war. Voting was the privilege of white men twenty-one years of age and older. "Women's place was in the home." Secretary Hay was on duty. John Nicolay, Lincoln's principal secretary, was in Illinois helping the Lincoln election campaign in the candidate's home state.

Men who were closely associated with the White House staff and who had not gone home to vote made themselves scarce on election day, seeming to be ashamed, and stayed away from the president.

Mr. Lincoln kept busy at the task of being president and commander-in-chief in time of civil war, remained in Washington, and worked in the White House all day. As a result, he could not vote, but it is probable that if he could have voted, he would not have voted for himself. In 1860, he had cut the presidential part of the ballot off the ticket rather than vote for himself. He had a feeling that it was not in good taste for a candidate to vote for himself.

The Republicans had renominated Mr. Lincoln on a Union ticket and had chosen Andrew Johnson, military governor of Tennessee, for vice-president. The Democrats had nominated Maj. Gen. George B. McClellan, who had commanded the Army of the Potomac and had been removed from command after the battle of Antietam for failing to follow up his victory by destroying Lee's army of Virginia and thus ending the war, a result that seemed at that time to be readily achievable.

Of this instance, the president had said, in September of 1864:

After the battle of Antietam, I went up to the field to try to get him (McClellan) to move and came back thinking he would move at once. But when I got home he began to argue why he ought not to move. I peremptorily ordered him to advance. It was 9 days longer before he got his army across and then he stopped again, delaying on little pretexts of wanting this and wanting that. I began to fear he was playing false—that he did not want to hurt the enemy. I saw how he could intercept the enemy on the way to Richmond. I determined to make the test. If he let them get away I would remove him. He did so and I relieved him.

McClellan's campaign for president was based on terminating the war. Lincoln's was based on winning the war.

The North was war weary, and clear up to about two weeks before the election, many of the Lincoln people thought that the president would be defeated.

Election day in Washington was rainy, and the weather added to the gloom.

During the day, Mr. Lincoln commented to John Hay, one of his secretaries, about the vindictiveness of the campaign and the vicious attacks made on him by his political opponents.

It is a little singular that I, who am not a vindictive man, should have always been before the people for election in canvasses marked for their bitterness; always but once; when I came to Congress it was a quiet time. But always besides that the contests in which I have been prominent have been marked with great rancor.

Around the country, there was great uncertainty, Senator Cameron of Pennsylvania, who had been relieved as secretary of war, was trying to get reelected to the Senate and was pushing his own campaign more than that for Lincoln, and the Union party was afraid it might lose the state. The New Yorkers were frightened; the Midwest was hard fought; all in all, the polling just might go wrong, so there was not much confidence around the White House. There were places where things looked good, but a great big "if" had to be added to every optimistic prediction. An estimate shown Mr. Lincoln indicated that he "might win" by twenty-one electoral votes, too close for comfort.

The president worked at his desk all day and had an

interview with a Mary E. Collins, a Southern lady, about a special exchange of Capt. William A. Collins of Co. D, 10th Wisconsin Infantry. Mr. Lincoln wrote to General Hitchcock, "Please see and hear this lady about a special exchange."

He recognized Teodoro Manara, who had just arrived to be consul of the republic of Guatemala at New York.

Tad, his son, had discovered that soldiers quartered in the White House grounds were voting for Lincoln and Johnson and prevailed upon his father to go to the window to watch.

At noon, the president discussed the election with Noah Brooks, an intimate friend and journalist whom he had known and trusted since his Illinois days, and then took time to receive from a man named Carlos Pierce an ox (the animal is described as "mammoth") named "General Grant." Mr. Lincoln donated the ox to the Sailor's Fair.

One of his callers was Whitelaw Reid, correspondent of the *Cincinnati Gazette,* who paid a short visit.

During the evening, Mr. Lincoln received the resignation of General McClellan as a major general in the Army. The resignation read strangely: "I have the honor to resign my commission as a Major General in the Army of the U.S., with the request that it take effect today. I am, sir, very respectfully, George B. McClellan."

Just why McClellan thought it an honor to resign and why he did it on the very day of the election in which he was running for president against President Lincoln are beyond me. I wish we knew Mr. Lincoln's reaction, but it is not recorded so far as I have learned.

With all this going on, Mr. Lincoln took time out to wire Secretary Seward, who had gone home to Auburn, New York, to vote, that "News from Grant, Sherman, Thomas and Rose-orans satisfactory but not important. Pirate *Florida* captured by U.S.S. *Mashusett* [which was misspelled in the wire]. This information is certain."

At noon, a dispatch had come from General Benjamin Butler, who had been sent to New York by Secretary Stanton because of rumors that election-day trouble might erupt into riots. The dispatch said that New York was "the quietest city ever seen." That relieved the tension somewhat. Incidentally, the president was not so concerned about New York as was

Secretary Stanton, and Mr. Lincoln had nothing to do with sending General Butler to keep the peace.

A dispatch came from Baltimore "giving a rose-coloured estimate of the fore-noon's voting there," and the President was cheered by the prospect.

But, as Hay's diary reveals, "during the afternoon few dispatches were received."

At seven o'clock that night, President Lincoln and John Hay started for the War Department to spend the evening alongside the telegraph keys, avid for news of the voting.

As he prepared to go to the War Department to receive election returns by telegraph, he put in his pocket a volume of the writings of the Toledo, Ohio, humorist David Ross Locke, who wrote under the non de plume Petroleum V. Nasby, and during lulls in the telegraph news, he read some of Nasby's humor, which was not appreciated by Secretary Stanton.

The very first message brought good news: Mr. Lincoln had carried Indianapolis by 8,000, and the news remained good and got better as the night wore on.

As Secretary Hay described the event,

The night was rainy, steamy and dark. We splashed through the grounds to the side door of the War Department where a soaked and smoking sentinel was standing in his own vapor with his huddled-up frame covered with a rubber cloak. Inside a half-dozen idle orderlies, up-stairs the clerks of the telegraph. As the President entered they handed him a dispatch from Forney claiming ten thousand majority in Philadelphia. "Forney is a little excitable." Another comes from Felton, Baltimore, giving us "15,000 in the city, 5,000 in the state. All Hail, Free Maryland." That is superb. A message from Rice to Assistant Secretary of the Navy Fox, followed instantly by one from Sumner to Lincoln, claiming Boston by 5,000 and Rice's and Hooper's elections by majorities of 4,000 apiece. A magnificent advance on the chilly dozens of 1862.

"Send these dispatches over to Mrs. Lincoln," the president said. "She is more anxious than I."

News came that Winter Davis, a Maryland congressman who had been particularly vindictive in his attacks on Mr. Lincoln, had been defeated, and there was general rejoicing.

Secretary of the Navy Wells, who had joined the party in Stanton's office, was particularly vocal in expressing his pleasure at Winter's downfall, as was Mr. Fox.

Fox said, "There are two fellows that have been especially malignant to us, and retribution has come upon them both, Hale and Winter Davis."

To which President Lincoln commented: "You have more of that feeling of personal resentment than I. Perhaps I may have too little of it but I never thought it paid. A man has not time to spend his life in quarrels. If any man ceases to attack me, I never remember the past against him."

The dispatches kept coming in.

A splendid triumph in Indiana.

Pennsylvania looking good instead of bad, as feared; Lincoln gaining all over the state.

New York still doubtful; the city seemingly may go 35,000 against Lincoln, leaving the state up in the air. General Butler wires McClellan may win the state by 40,000.

Massachusetts 80,000 for Lincoln.

Maryland, Lincoln by 10,000.

Another from New York, now claiming the state for Lincoln by 40,000. The final vote was 5,000 for Lincoln.

Illinois, 25,000 for Lincoln.

And so it went through the long evening until about midnight when supper was served. The principal dish was fried oysters, and Hay says, "The President went awkwardly and hospitably to work shoveling out the fried oysters."

One of the men complained that the coffee was too hot!

And all through the supper interlude, the dispatches kept coming, and as the telegraph keys clicked with good news, the watchers became jubilant with the expectation of victory.

Michigan for Lincoln.

Missouri for Lincoln.

At about half past two, an army band arrived in the rain, under a Captain Thomas, and serenaded the victorious president, who opened the window, and expressed his thanks to the band and his appreciation of the confidence of the people.

So went election night 1864 for Abraham Lincoln of Illinois, the first president since Andrew Jackson to be reelected. The people had spoken, and the people wanted the war won and wanted Mr. Lincoln for four more years.

How did that rainy day turn out for the United States and for Abraham Lincoln? He received 221 votes in the Electoral College to 21 for General McClellan, who carried only New Jersey, Delaware, and Kentucky. It was a resounding Lincoln victory.

The *Washington Star* of November ninth carried the banner headline "Abraham Lincoln has been elected by an overwhelming majority."

On November eleventh, the Cabinet met, and President Lincoln opened the meeting by going to his desk and taking out a paper.

Let John Hay tell the story from his diary:

The President said: "Gentlemen, do you remember last summer I asked you all to sign your names to the back of a paper of which I did not show you the inside? This is it. Now, Mr. Hay, see if you can get this open without tearing it?" He had pasted it up in so singular style that it required cutting to get it open. He then read as follows:

Executive Mansion
Washington, Aug. 23, 1864
"This morning, as for some days past, it seems exceedingly probable that this administration will not be re-elected. Then it will be my duty to so co-operate with the President-elect as to save the Union between the election and inauguration day; as he will have secured his election on such ground that he cannot possibly save it afterward."

A. Lincoln

This was endorsed:
William H. Seward
W. P. Fessenden
Edwin M. Stanton
Gideon Wells
Edwd Bates
M. Blair
J. P. Usher
August 23, 1864
The President said, "You will remember that this was written at a time (6 days before the Chicago nominating Convention) when as

82

yet we had no adversary, and seemed to have no friends. I then solemnly resolved on the course of action indicated above. I resolved, in case of the election of General McClellan, being certain that he would be the candidate, that I would see him and talk matters over with him. I would say, "General, the election has demonstrated that you are stronger, have more influence with the American people than I. Now let us together, you with your influence and I with all the executive power of the Government, try to save the country. You raise as many troops as you possibly can for this final trial, and I will devote all my energies to assisting and finishing the war."

Seward said, "And the General would answer you 'Yes, Yes,' and the next day when you saw him again and pressed these views upon him, he would say, 'Yes, Yes,' & so on forever, and would have done nothing at all."

"At least," added Lincoln, "I should have done my duty and have stood clear before my own conscience."

PART THREE

Postassassination

Tragedy Begets Tragedy

When Clara Harris and Henry Rathbone left the Washington home of her father, Sen. Ira Harris of New York, at eight fifteen on the night of April 14, 1865, they were a very happy couple, and apparently they had every reason so to be.

The Civil War had practically ended. Lee had surrendered the Army of Northern Virginia to Grant at Appomattox, and all that was left to be done to conclude hostilities was for Sherman's great army marching north through the Carolinas to "mop up" the dejected Confederate troops under command of Gen. Joseph E. Johnston, whose surrender came twelve days later. The nation was wild with joy, and they shared in the relief and happiness that was universal in the North on that night.

They had an even greater reason for happiness. Although Major Rathbone was Miss Harris's stepbrother, they had fallen in love with each other and were engaged to be married.

That afternoon, they had received an invitation from President and Mrs. Lincoln to attend the theater that night, and they looked forward to a historic evening of joy and excitement.

Life looked bright, indeed, for those young people that night.

But tragedy was to becloud their happiness in a very short time after they entered the presidential carriage, and it was to stalk them to the end of their lives.

When Booth entered the Lincoln box at the theater and shot the president, Rathbone threw himself at the assassin.

Booth wounded him with a dagger, leaped from the box onto the stage, and fled through the stage door into an alley where a "half-witted boy," John "Peanuts" Burroughs, was holding a horse for him. Knocking the boy aside, Booth, although limping from a broken leg, was able to leap on the horse and gallop off into the darkness.

The wounded Major Rathbone secured medical aid after he and Miss Harris had done their best to attend Mrs. Lincoln in the hectic hours after the assassination, and they returned to the Harris home. Subsequently, they were interrogated, of course, by officials preparing for the trial of the conspirators.

Sometime after the assassination, they were married. But happiness was not to be theirs. As Lorant describes it, Clara Harris's "end, like that of all the others who occupied the box that night, was tragic—Rathbone, a raving madman, killed her."

The Faithless
Guard

Of the myriad men whose names appear in the five-point footnotes of history, that of John F. Parker deserves much more than passing attention. This little-known man had an influence on his country and his own and future generations far beyond that of most Americans, including presidents and legislators and educators and other public figures. Yet few among the two hundred plus millions who inhabit this country today know that he existed.

Ask a dozen of your acquaintances: "What do you know about John F. Parker of Washington, D.C.?" and I'll be surprised if any knows anything about him. Yet what he did and his infidelity to duty made possible—indeed, was directly responsible—for the assassination of President Abraham Lincoln.

If John F. Parker had done his duty on the night of April 14, 1865, the slaying of Abraham Lincoln could have been—probably would have been—prevented, and had Lincoln lived, served out his second term as president, the future of America would have been vastly different from that which history records.

Parker is in no way accused of being part of the conspiracy organized by John Wilkes Booth, but his default in duty was as certain a condition resulting in the murder of Lincoln as though he had plotted and organized the crime.

Booth, on learning from reading the newspapers that Mr. Lincoln would attend Ford's theater on April 14, 1865, made elaborate preparation to slay the president. He visited the theater, where he was a familiar figure as an actor, drilled a hole in the door of the box the president would occupy so he could see those sitting there, and then cut an indentation in the wall by the door inside the hallway leading to the box so he could, by wedging a heavy board as a bar to opening the door, prevent anyone from entering the passageway leading to the presidential box. By this device, he had a clear field and undisturbed time in which to commit his crime.

Between the door that Booth planned to bar and the door to the box, the theater management placed a chair to be used by the armed guard who was stationed there and whose duty it was to prevent any unauthorized person from entering the presidential box.

As Booth's plan provided, if he could gain admission to the door opening into the corridor leading to the box and then bar it with his wedge of wood to prevent its being opened, he could observe the president and his party through the "peep hole" and wait, without hindrance, until he was ready to enter and fire the fatal shot.

Had guard Parker stayed on duty at his post, Booth's plan would have failed. The only way he could have gained admission would have been by overpowering Parker, and the noise incident to that could have aroused so many people that the actor could not have gotten to the president.

Carl Sandburg in *Lincoln, the War Years* writes, "How he (Parker) found his way into the White House to begin with is not clear from the records." It seems certain, though, that he was assigned to the White House duty by the newly created Metropolitan Police Force.

When Parker was about to be drafted for army service, Mrs. Lincoln intervened on his behalf, writing to the provost marshal of the District of Columbia that "John F. Parker . . . has been detailed for duty at the Executive Mansion by order of Mrs. Lincoln." It was signed by Mrs. Lincoln. She wrote, instead of the president, to retain Parker as a guard, thus preventing his being drafted, because Mr. Lincoln at that time (probably April 3) was in Petersburg, Virginia. Parker had previously served one enlistment during the war. Several of the White House staff had been drafted, and it is presumed that the Lincolns, seeing the war approaching its end, wished to avoid "breaking in" a new attaché. Hence, the letter.

On the night of April 14, President Lincoln had indicated that he would be satisfied with the protection of Charles Forbes, his footman, and of Parker, detailed from the Metropolitan Police. White House guard William H. Crook, who generally accompanied Lincoln for protective purposes, offered to serve on duty that night, but the president was quite willing to excuse Crook and to be "content" with Parker.

After the assassination, Crook said that he gave Parker strict and specific orders to watch over the Lincolns and their guests from their carriage to their box in the theater and then to stand, fully armed, in the vestibule leading to the box and to keep any unauthorized person from entering the vestibule.

After the assassination, Parker told Crook that when the first act of the play, *An American Cousin*, was finished, presidential coachman Burke, footman Forbes, and he (Parker) went out together to get a drink and were gone for at least ten minutes. When they returned, Parker took a seat in "the dress circle" to watch the balance of the play. No one was guarding Abraham Lincoln.

On May 1, 1865, Parker was charged with neglect of duty by Superintendent Richards of the Metropolitan Police. The charge specified that Parker was detailed to attend and protect the president while he was at Ford's Theatre on the night of the 14th of April 1865 and accused Parker of allowing a man to enter the box and shoot Mr. Lincoln.

Two witnesses were named: Superintendent Richards and footman Forbes.

The board of the Metropolitan Police tried Parker the afternoon of May 3, the hearing being held at the board offices, 483 Tenth Street.

Records of the trial are missing from the police department's files, which are described as having "suffered through past lack of adequate housing and custody."

The trial was held *in camera* after the custom in such

91

procedures in those times. The complaint was dismissed on June 2, 1865. So far as I can tell no one living today knows what occurred at the hearing.

Guard Crook commented that Parker "looked like a convicted criminal" after the trial and "was never the same man afterward."

Parker remained on the Metropolitan force until 1868 when he was dismissed for sleeping on duty.

What became of John F. Parker? He seems to have dropped from sight after 1868. What a tormented life he must have lived with the knowledge that had he been faithful to duty on April 14, he probably could have saved Lincoln's life! What did remorse do to his character? Does he have descendants? These and many more questions naturally occur to an even casually interested person. They remain unanswered. The only explanation is that he disappeared into the mainstream of Washington's thousands of "faceless" people and wandered about during the balance of his life; surely he must have been overwhelmed by a crushing weight of guilt.

The record ends with his dismissal in 1868.

Had he been a soldier instead of a policeman on duty in Ford's theater, his fate would have been a firing squad.

Perhaps Parker, who had to live with his crime of neglect of duty, paid a penalty in an unbearable weight of conscience that was worse than death. Such would have been a fitting sentence.

Official Congressional Reaction to the Assassination

Senators and representatives who were in Washington at the time of the assassination of President Lincoln (he was shot on the night of Good Friday, April 14, 1865, and died the next morning at 7:22 o'clock) gathered in the reception room at the Capitol on Monday, April 17, the first business day after the tragedy.

The gathering was of necessity an unofficial one because Congress was in recess. Those present were in a state of grief and shock, and they met to provide for congressional participation in the funeral arrangements.

The usual cold, dispassionate governmental prose of the official record cannot prevent the grief and shocked emotions of those in attendance from revealing itself. Even after the passage of more than a quarter of a century, the sadness of the occasion shows through these words, written by a grieving scribe. The record follows:

ACTION OF SENATORS AND REPRESENTATIVES IN WASHINGTON.

[From Appendix to Memorial Address on the Life and Character of Abraham Lincoln.]

The members of the Thirty-ninth Congress then in Washington met in the Senate reception room, at the Capitol, on the 17th of April, 1865, at noon. Hon. Lafayette S. Foster, of Connecticut, President *pro tempore* of the Senate, was called to the chair, and the Hon. Schuyler Colfax, of Indiana, Speaker of the House in the Thirty-eighth Congress, was chosen secretary.

Senator Foot, of Vermont, who was visibly affected, stated that the object of the meeting was to make arrangements relative to the funeral of the deceased President of the United States.

On motion of Senator Sumner, of Massachusetts, a committee of five members from each House was ordered to report at 4 p.m. what action would be fitting for the meeting to take.

The chairman appointed Senators Sumner, of Massachusetts; Harris, of New York; Johnson, of Maryland; Ramsey, of Minnesota, and Conness, of California, and Representatives Washburne, of Illinois; Smith, of Kentucky; Schenck, of Ohio; Pike, of Maine, and Coffroth, of Pennsylvania; and on motion of Mr. Schenck the chairman and secretary of the meeting were added to the committee, and then the meeting adjourned until 4 p.m.

The meeting reassembled ar 4 P.M., pursuant to adjournment.

Mr. Sumner, from the committee heretofore appointed, reported that they had selected as pallbearers on the part of the Senate Mr. Foster, of Connecticut; Mr. Morgan, of New York; Mr. Johnson, of Maryland; Mr. Yates, of Illinois; Mr. Wade, of Ohio, and Mr. Conness, of California; on the part of the House, Mr. Dawes, of Massachusetts; Mr. Coffroth, of Pennsylvania; Mr. Smith, of Kentucky; Mr. Colfax, of Indiana; Mr. Worthington, of Nevada, and Mr. Washburne, of Illinois.

They also recommended the appointment of one member of Congress from each State and Territory to act as a Congressional committee to accompany the remains of the late President to Illinois, and presented the following names as such committee, the chairman of the meeting to have the authority of appointing hereafter for the States and Territories not represented to-day from which members may be present at the Capitol by the day of the funeral.

Maine, Mr. Pike; New Hampshire, Mr. E. H. Rollins; Vermont, Mr. Foot; Massachusetts, Mr. Sumner; Rhode Island, Mr. Anthony; Connecticut, Mr. Dixon; New York, Mr. Harris; Pennsylvania, Mr. Cowan; Ohio, Mr. Schenck; Kentucky, Mr. Smith; Indiana, Mr. Julian; Illinois, the delegation; Michigan, Mr. Chandler; Iowa, Mr. Harlan; California, Mr. Shannon; Minnesota, Mr. Ramsey; Oregon, Mr. Williams; Kansas, Mr. S. Clarke; West Virginia, Mr. Whaley; Nevada, Mr. Nye; Nebraska, Mr. Hitchcock; Colorado, Mr. Bradford; Dakota, Mr. Todd; Idaho, Mr. Wallace.

The committee also recommended the adoption of the following resolution:

Resolved, That the Sergeants-at-Arms of the Senate and House, with their necessary assistants, be requested to attend the committee accompanying the remains of the late President, and to make all the necessary arrangements.

All of which was concurred in unanimously.

Mr. Sumner, from the same committee, also reported the following, which was unanimously agreed to:

The members of the Senate and House of Representatives now assembled in Washington, humbly confessing their dependence upon Almighty God, who rules all that is done for human good, make haste at this informal meeting to express the emotions with which they have been filled by the appalling tragedy which has deprived the nation of its head and covered the land with mourning; and in further declaration of their sentiments unanimously resolve:

1. That in testimony of their veneration and affection for the illustrious dead, who has been permitted, under Providence, to do so much for his country and for liberty, they will unite in the funeral services and by an appropriate committee will accompany his remains to their place of burial in the State from which he was taken for the national service.

2. That in the life of Abraham Lincoln, who by the benignant favor of republican institutions rose from humble beginnings to the heights of power and fame, they recognize an example of purity, simplicity, and virtue which should be a lesson to mankind, while in his death they recognize a martyr whose memory will become more precious as men learn to prize those principles of constitutional order and those rights—civil, political, and human—for which he was made a sacrifice.

3. That they invite the President of the United States, by solemn proclamation, to recommend to the people of the United States to assemble on a day to be appointed by him, publicly to testify their grief and to dwell on the good which has been done on earth by him whom we now mourn.

4. That a copy of these resolutions be communicated to the President of the United States, and also that a copy be communicated to the afflicted widow of the late President as an expression of sympathy in her great bereavement.

The meeting then adjourned.

Lincoln's Lone Descendant

Robert Todd Lincoln Beckwith of Washington, D.C., is, at this writing (1978), the only living direct descendant of Abraham Lincoln. On July 10, 1975, Mr. Beckwith's sister, May Beckwith, died at her home in Vermont. Her death left her brother the sole descendant of the president. Robert T. L. and May Beckwith were the children of Jessie Lincoln, one of two daughters of Robert Todd Lincoln, the president's oldest child.

The president had four sons: Robert (1843–1926), Edward (1846–1850), William (1850–1862), and Thomas (Tad; 1853–1871).

Robert Todd Lincoln was the only one of the president's four sons to live to maturity and marriage. He married Mary Harlan, daughter of U.S. Sen. James Harlan of Iowa, and they had three children.

Robert Lincoln's first child, Mary, born in 1869, married Charles Isham, by whom she bore a son, Lincoln Isham, in 1892. Lincoln Isham died in 1971.

The second child, Abraham Lincoln, II, was born in 1873. He was known as "Jack" by the family and close friends. He died in London on March 5, 1890, during Robert Todd Lincoln's term as United States minister to the Court of St. James's.

Robert T. Lincoln's third child, Jessie, was born in 1875 and died in 1948. She married Warren Beckwith in 1897, and they had two children, Mary (May), born in 1898 (May's death is referred to in the first paragraph of this chapter), and Robert Todd Lincoln Beckwith, born July 19, 1904.

The accompanying chart shows the descendants of Abraham and Mary Todd Lincoln

In its story of July 11, 1975, in which it told of the death of Mary (May) Todd Lincoln Beckwith, United Press International reported as follows:

Manchester, Vt. (UPI)—Miss Mary Todd Lincoln Beckwith, 77, died Thursday at Rutland Hospital.

She was the granddaughter of Robert Todd Lincoln, the son of Abraham Lincoln, the nation's 16th President, and his wife, Mary Todd Lincoln.

Miss Beckwith requested in her will that her ashes be spread over her estate. That request will be fulfilled.

Since 1938, she had operated her grandfather's 1,000-acre summer estate known as Hildene. Miss Beckwith was shy of publicity, but was loved by her friends and neighbors.

In its prime, her estate had horse stables and she had developed a reputation for her horsemanship. At one time, she ran a dairy farm which she farmed with the help of hired hands.

At her request there will be no funeral or memorial service.

Miss Beckwith's will provided that the estate ultimately should go to the Mother Church of Christ, Scientist, Boston, Massachusetts.

A news item in the *Cincinnati Post* of August 6, 1976, detailed a sad circumstance in the life of Robert Todd Lincoln Beckwith:

The estranged wife of Robert Todd Lincoln Beckwith, 71, the great-grandson of Abraham Lincoln, will appeal a divorce Beckwith won in a District of Columbia court because she was not allowed to present her case. Beckwith was awarded the divorce on grounds of adultery this week from Annemarie Hoffman Beckwith, 35, who did not attend the two-day trial and faces contempt citations in connection with the case.

Testimony by doctors showed Beckwith could not have fathered his estranged wife's 7-year-old son, Timothy Lincoln Beckwith, because he had undergone a vasectomy six years before the boy was born. The son, however, still may hold a claim to the Lincoln estate, estimated to be about $1 million, because of an earlier court ruling which specified that regardless of the outcome of the case, the child would not be bound on the paternity suit.

The Lincoln trust, established by Lincoln's son, Robert Todd,

ABRAHAM LINCOLN AND MARY TODD
(MARRIED NOVEMBER 4, 1842)

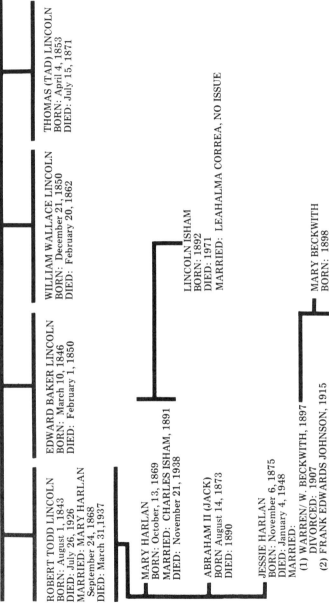

THOMAS (TAD) LINCOLN
BORN: April 4, 1853
DIED: July 15, 1871

WILLIAM WALLACE LINCOLN
BORN: December 21, 1850
DIED: February 20, 1862

LINCOLN ISHAM
BORN: 1892
DIED: 1971
MARRIED: LEAHALMA CORREA, NO ISSUE

EDWARD BAKER LINCOLN
BORN: March 10, 1846
DIED: February 1, 1850

MARY BECKWITH
BORN: 1898
DIED: 1975

ROBERT LINCOLN BECKWITH
BORN: July 19, 1904

ROBERT TODD LINCOLN
BORN: August 1, 1843
DIED: July 26, 1926
MARRIED: MARY HARLAN
    September 24, 1868
DIED: March 31, 1937

MARY HARLAN
BORN: October, 13, 1869
MARRIED: CHARLES ISHAM, 1891
DIED: November 21, 1938

ABRAHAM II (JACK)
BORN August 14, 1873
DIED: 1890

JESSIE HARLAN
BORN: November 6, 1875
DIED: January 4, 1948
MARRIED:
    (1) WARREN/W. BECKWITH, 1897
        DIVORCED: 1907
    (2) FRANK EDWARDS JOHNSON, 1915
        DIVORCED: 1916
    (3) ROBERT J. RANDOLPH, 1917
        DIED:

provides that after Beckwith's death, the estate should be equally divided among the First Church of Christ Scientist in Boston, the American National Red Cross and Iowa Wesleyan College.

The appeal in the divorce case is from the District of Columbia Family Division Court, which held in favor of Mr. Beckwith, to the District of Columbia Court of Appeals and was heard on April 20, 1977. Mr. Beckwith's divorce was validated. The question of a claim on the estate is still before the courts.

Things Mr. Lincoln Said
and
Things He Did Not Say

Literature and folklore about Mr. Lincoln are replete with statements he made about people, institutions, and human actions. Some of them are true; he said them. Many are untrue; he did not say them. Some of the stories, repeated again and again, have been altered from his original statement, sometimes by careless repetition and sometimes to bend his remarks to suit the ideas or the causes of the teller.

In this chapter, the spotlight of research is used to tell some of the things he said and some he didn't say.

MR. LINCOLN SAID IT:
IS GOVERNMENT PERPETUAL?

I hold, that in contemplation of universal law, and of the Constitution, the Union of these states is perpetual. Perpetuity is implied, if not expressed, in the fundamental law of all national governments. It is safe to assert that no government proper ever had a provision in its organic law for its own termination. Continue to execute all of the express provisions of our national constitution and the Union will endure forever—it being impossible to destroy it, except for some action not provided in the instrument itself.

RULE OF MINORITY WHOLLY INADMISSIBLE

A majority, held in restraint by constitutional checks, and limitations, and always changing easily, with deliberate changes of popular opinions and sentiments, is the only true sovereign of a free people. Unanimity is impossible; the rule of a minority, as a permanent arrangement, is wholly inadmissible; so that, rejecting the majority principal, anarchy, or despotism in some form, is all that is left.

DANGER OF RULE BY SUPREME COURT

At the same time the candid citizen must confess that *if* the policy of the government upon vital questions, affecting the whole people, is to be irrevocably fixed by decisions of the Supreme Court, the instant they are made, in ordinary litigation between parties, in personal actions, the will of the people will have ceased, to be their own rulers, having, to that extent, practically resigned their government into the hands of that eminent tribunal.

VIRTUE AND VIGILANCE CAN PREVENT GOVERNMENTAL FOLLY

While the people retain their virtue, and vigilance, no administration, by any extreme of wickedness or folly, can very seriously injure the government in the short space of four years.
(*N.B.:* The above quotations are from Mr. Lincoln's first inaugural address delivered on March 4, 1861.)

WHAT HAPPENS WHEN GOVERNMENT LIVES BY BORROWING?

On March 4, 1843, Mr. Lincoln wrote a circular for the Whig Party in which he makes this comment on the government borrowing money:

An individual who undertakes to live by borrowing soon finds his original means devoured by interest and, next, no one left to borrow from—so must it be with a government.

MR. LINCOLN DID NOT SAY IT:
WHAT LINCOLN REALLY SAID ABOUT THE COMMON PEOPLE

Mr. Lincoln often is quoted as saying, "The Lord must have loved the common people; he made so many of them."

101

Did he say it? Research shows that he did not.

The legend grew out of an anecdote told by John Hay, one of his secretaries, and is to be found on page 143 of *The Letters of John Hay*.

Here is Hay's account:

The President last night (December 22, 1863) had a dream.

He was in a party of plain people and as it became known who he was they began to comment on his appearance. One of them said: "He is a very common looking man." The President replied, "Common *looking* people are the best in the world; that is the reason the Lord makes so many of them."

Waking, he remembered it and told it as a neat thing.

"TOTALLY UNTRUE"

Over many years, I have seen and heard the following statement ascribed to President Lincoln:

You cannot bring about prosperity by discouraging thrift. You cannot strengthen the weak by weakening the strong. You cannot help the wage earner by pulling down the wage payer. You cannot further the brotherhood of many by encouraging class hatred. You cannot help the poor by discouraging the rich. You cannot establish sound security on borrowed money. You cannot keep out of trouble by spending more than you earn. You cannot build character and courage by taking away man's initiative and independence. You cannot help men permanently by doing for them what they could and should do for themselves.

I searched my Lincoln library and my voluminous files on Lincoln statements in a vain effort to authenticate the so-called quotation.

I consulted recognized authorities, and two of the most reliable and prestigious say categorically that Lincoln did not make this statement.

Dr. William K. Alderfer, secretary of the Abraham Lincoln Association, Springfield, Illinois, responding to my inquiry about the statement, wrote:

The statement in your letter of March 10, 1975, attributed to Abraham Lincoln is totally untrue. I do not know who sends these mis-statements to you but evidently they have not researched the Lincoln papers.

Answering a similar letter from me inquiring as to the authenticity of this and another statement attributed to Lincoln, Dr. Mark E. Neely, director of the Lincoln National Life Foundation in Fort Wayne, Indiana, labeled both as "spurious" and included material from *Lincoln Lore,* a very responsible publication of the Foundation, which, in its issue of January 1962, under the heading "Lincoln Never Said That," carried the following:

Editor's Note: Nearly every week since 1949 several letters are addressed to the Lincoln National Life Foundation inquiring about the authenticity of the "You Cannot . . ." axioms attributed to Abraham Lincoln. In Lincoln Lore, Number 1085, January 23, 1950, "Axioms Credited to Lincoln, Unauthentic," the editor of the bulletin attempted to settle once and for all the fact that Lincoln was not the author of the ten point quotation. However, the brand "spurious" has not checked the growing interest in the axioms.

In order that attention may again be focused on the spurious claim of authorship the above mentioned Lincoln Lore is reprinted. However, since this issue of Lincoln Lore was published in 1950, it has been discovered that the Rev. William J. H. Boetcker of Erie, Pennsylvania wrote the axioms and that they were first published by him in 1916. He also used them in other pamphlets in 1917, 1938 and 1945. In 1942 the ten axioms were published by the Committee for Constitutional Government with the credit line "Inspiration of Wm. J. H. Boetcker" with an authentic quotation of Abraham Lincoln on the other side of the sheet entitled "Lincoln on Limitation." When a larger edition of the leaflet was printed by the committee they left off the name Boetcker. This and subsequent editions were then published which lead readers to assume that the words of both sides of the sheet were the words of Lincoln.

The arresting title of this editor's note "Lincoln Never Said That" is borrowed from Albert A. Woldman's article that appeared in Harper's Magazine for May 1950. Woldman wrote, "There was no reason for Lincoln to say any of these things . . . the words do not ring true. . . . They were made to order for present day consumption."

This misquotation dies hard, but even though one may subscribe to the thought of the "you cannots," it should not be attributed to Mr. Lincoln.

Prohibition

As an illustration of how far people have gone—and, I believe, will go in the future—to aid some "cause" in which they are espousing by ascribing bogus statements to Mr. Lincoln, I quote the following from *Lincoln Lore*, issue of November 6, 1939:

Whenever the prohibition question is brought to the front the following statement said to have been made by Lincoln is often quoted:

"Prohibition will work great injury to the cause of temperance. It is a species of intemperance itself for it goes beyond the bounds of reason in that it attempts to control man's appetite by legislation in making crimes out of things that are not crimes. A prohibitory law strikes a blow at the very principles on which our government was founded. I have always been found laboring to protect the weaker classes from the stronger and I can never give my consent to such a law as you propose to enact. Until my tongue be silenced in death I will continue to fight for the rights of man."

Atlanta, Georgia, was in the midst of a local option campaign in 1887, and the alleged Lincoln statement above was widely circulated in the campaign.

Some time after the excitement of the campaign had disappeared, Colonel Samuel W. Small was told by Colonel John B. Goodwin, who had been the director of the AntiProhibition forces, that he himself composed the alleged words of Lincoln to influence the colored voters to vote the wet ticket.

About Fooling the People

Another famous statement credited to Mr. Lincoln for which there is no documentary evidence is this one:

You can fool all the people some of the time
And some of the people all the time,
But you cannot fool all the people all the time.

While a survey taken in 1905 by the *Brooklyn Eagle* produced some people who claimed to have heard Mr. Lincoln make that statement in a speech at Clinton, Illinois, in 1858, it is not found in any of Mr. Lincoln's printed speeches or in

104

any of his writings, and careful researchers doubt its authenticity.

There also is grave doubt that he ever said, "I'll study and get ready and then my chance will come," or the more familiar version: "I will study and prepare myself and one day my chance will come."

MR. LINCOLN INVESTS
SAVINGS FROM SALARY

In June of 1864 Mr. Lincoln discussed with Secretary of the Treasury Chase a personal investment problem. He had accumulated more than $50,000.00 and needed to get it invested. Like many presidents he felt that he had to be extremely careful about investments. For example, if it got out that the President of the United States has invested in certain stocks or bonds, others might be induced to invest in the same securities, feeling that the President might have inside information on a good thing. Among modern presidents two that I know about had the same feeling.

President Harding would invest in nothing but government bonds and whenever his salary accumulated Mr. Charles E. Hard of the White House staff would go to the treasury and buy government bonds directly from Secretary of the Treasury Andrew Mellon. At the time of the transaction Mr. Mellon would accept the funds for investment from Mr. Hard and painstakingly write a receipt in his own handwriting.

Just before President Kennedy assumed office he placed his wealth in a trust fund invested in municipal bonds.

Mr. Lincoln took his savings in 1864 directly to Secretary Chase, with the letter, a photocopy of which appears herein. As he noted on the bottom of the letter he: "Left with Gov. Chase to fix up for me this 11 June, 1864."

Executive Mansion.

Washington. June 10   1864.

Hon. Sec. of Treasury
    My dear Sir

            Herewith are the documents which
you kindly proposed fixing up for me, towit.

1	Treasurers receipt, of March 15. 1862. of 7 30's	$14. 200.
2	do do April 16. do " "	" 2.000.00
3	Certificate of Deposits, Aug 1. 1863.	" 22.306.67
4	do do " 18. do	" 3.874.73
5.	5—20's	" 8 000.00.
6,	Two Warrents $2022 33/, $2025 14/100	4044.67
7.	Greenbacks.	89.00.
		54,515·07

Left with Gov. Chase to fix up on
th. 11. June 1864

Lincoln's memorandum of savings from his salary as President.   Courtesy of Illinois State Historical Library and Society.

Potpourri—Lloyd's "Lincoln Notebook"

For many years I have kept a "Lincoln notebook" wherein are written, pasted, and clipped a mass (which I never have counted) of items, anecdotes, and incidents about Abraham Lincoln and his life that I have found to be interesting.

This chapter contains a random sampling gathered while "rambling through" Lloyd's "Lincoln Notebook." I have been able to authenticate each. My hope is that you, also, may find them interesting.

"WORTH MORE THAN A BATTLE WON"

General Grant was so cheered by news of Lincoln's reelection that he wired the president: "The victory was worth more than a battle won."

YOUNG ARMY SURGEON KEEPS DATE WITH DESTINY

On March 1, 1865, Charles A. Leale received his doctor of medicine degree from Bellevue Hospital Medical College in New York City.

On March 26, 1865, Dr. Leale celebrated his twenty-third birthday anniversary.

On April 10, 1865, Dr. Leale took the oath of office as an acting assistant surgeon in the Union Army.

On April 14, 1865, just over a month after "becoming" a doctor of medicine, Leale was the first physician to reach

Abraham Lincoln after the president was shot by John Wilkes Booth.

On that Good Friday, Dr. Leale, having learned that the president would attend Ford's Theatre that night, changed from Army uniform into civilian cloths and went to Ford's Theatre. He purchased a ticket and, entering the theatre, found to his delight that it was located in the dress circle on the same side of the theatre as the presidential box.

It was a desire to "see the president again" (the doctor having heard Mr. Lincoln speak from a window of the White House a few nights before and having been impressed greatly both by the man and his message) that attracted Leale to the theater, not the play or Laura Keane, the star.

As soon as he realized that the president had been shot, Leale climbed into the presidential box, identified himself as an army surgeon, and began to attend the president, who was sitting slumped over in his chair with his head against the wall.

Leale and Major Rathbone removed the wounded president from his chair and placed him on the floor. Dr. Leale then administered mouth-to-mouth resuscitation, which was effective in restoring normal breathing, and removed a clot of blood from the open wound where the bullet had entered the back of the head. As long as the wound was free from clotting, the patient rested relatively easily.

It was Dr. Leale who supervised the removal of the president to the Peterson house across the street, and he attended him until death occurred at 7:22 the next morning. Other physicians came and assisted. The president died without recovering consciousness.

As an expression of the Lincoln family's appreciation of Dr. Leale's services, he was assigned a place of honor at the head of the coffin in the public funeral at the Capitol and rode in the carriage immediately preceding the coffin in the procession from the White House to the Capitol.

Dr. Leale never removed the crepe from the sword he wore at the funeral and saved his cuffs that had been stained with Mr. Lincoln's blood. The doctor died in 1932, having practiced general medicine throughout his life.

No Life Insurance

There is no record of President Lincoln's ever having owned life insurance, and my inquiries among life insurance companies that were in existence during his lifetime failed to show him as a purchaser.

The Lincoln home in Springfield was insured against damage by fire in a policy that he purchased from the Hartford Fire Insurance Company.

Wore Glasses for Close Vision

Mr. Lincoln wore glasses for close vision, reading, writing, etc., and purchased them from a Washington firm, Franklin & Co., which made them to conform to a doctor's prescription.

Before his nomination, he used, for a while, a pince-nez, which he carried on a black silk ribbon worn about his neck.

It is probable that these were the glasses he used at the time he delivered the famous address at Cooper Union Institute in New York on February 27, 1860, a speech that created favorable comment throughout the North and made him well known in New York and New England. Mr. Lincoln received an honorarium of $200 for making that address, and the Institute paid his expenses.

After his speech he made a tour of New England, speaking in Hartford and New Haven in Connecticut and visiting his son, Robert, who was a student at Phillips Exeter Academy in Exeter, New Hampshire, doing preparatory work to qualify him for entrance to Harvard.

Mr. Lincoln spent the night of March 5, 1860, as the guest of Governor William A. Buckingham of Connecticut. Mr. Buckingham served in that office, so the present governor, Hon. Ella Grasso, kindly wrote me, from 1858 to 1866.

Lincoln left his nose glasses and the ribbon at the governor's house, and they were preserved by the governor and his family. A few years ago, a member of the family gave the glasses and the ribbon to the Lincoln Library and

Museum in Springfield, Illinois, where they may be seen in a glass case in the museum in the Old Capitol.

During his New England tour, Mr. Lincoln spoke in Providence, Rhode Island, Dover, New Hampshire, Exeter, New Hampshire, Concord, New Hampshire, and Manchester, New Hampshire.

JUST A COINCIDENCE?

On the ninth of November, 1863, a minor, ironic event took place in Washington. President Lincoln attended a theater and watched John Wilkes Booth play the leading role in a drama entitled *Marble Heart.*

In another theater, Ford's, 521 days later, Booth assassinated Lincoln.

In the theater party on November 9, 1863, were the president, Mrs. Lincoln, a Mrs. Hunter, former Secretary of War Cameron, and Lincoln's secretaries, John Nicolay and John Hay.

Hay, commenting in his diary, says of the play: "Rather tame than otherwise."

Two days later, Hay and three others saw Booth play Romeo in Shakespeare's *Romeo and Juliet* in the same theatre. Commenting on the play, Hay confided to his diary that "Wheatley (another actor in the play) took all the honors away as Mercurio."

MARFAN'S SYNDROME

A physical condition known as Marfan's syndrome was first identified by a French physician, Dr. B. J. A. Marfan, in 1896. It is described in the 1963 November-December issue of *Spectrum* (a medical journal) as "a protein disorder that has repercussions throughout the body. Skeletal, ocular, and cardiovascular abnormalities are its most familiar manifestations. . . ."

Dr. T. R. Van Dellen, prominent medical columnist for newspapers, answering, "a nurse in Terre Haute, Ind." who inquired whether Mr. Lincoln had the disease and "would it have hampered his ability as a president?" wrote:

It does appear likely that President Lincoln had Marfan's disease. This is a hereditary condition that was first described in France several decades after Lincoln died. Patients with this condition are often tall and lanky, with very long fingers and large hands and feet. Frequently they are double-jointed and can bend their elongated extremities into unusual positions.

Often the face is long and sad in appearance; the ears may be large and the chin protrudes—a rather accurate description of Lincoln's facial appearance. Marfan patients often have an awkward appearance because of their slouching posture, their flat feet and the very little fat under their skin.

Other abnormalities may include dislocation of the lens of the eyes; hernias, and dilation of the aorta, the large blood vessel leading from the heart.

Photographs and descriptions of Lincoln indicate that he had many of these characteristics. His mother also was similarly affected.

Did it affect his ability? Not in my opinion. I think most historians agree that Lincoln was one of our greatest presidents and leaders. If he did have Marfan's disease, he is by far the most famous of its victims.

Lloyd Spies for Lincoln

Interesting to me because of the similarity in names is the life of a man named William Alvin Lloyd, who served President Lincoln as an undercover intelligence agent throughout the South in the early days of the Civil War.

As nearly as I can verify the story, William Alvin Lloyd, who had business interests in New York and Baltimore was a publisher of railroad and steamboat guides and maps of the Southern states, came to President Lincoln with a request for a pass through the army lines so that he could pursue his business affairs in the South.

Apparently, the president saw his opportunity to recruit an undercover agent who would make intelligence reports directly to the president. He seized the opportunity, and Lloyd agreed to furnish Mr. Lincoln all the information he could garner on Confederate troop movements, railroad and steamship matters, and any other information he could come across during his travels as a businessman pursuing his normal avocation. Mr. Lincoln agreed to pay him $200 a month and gave him a pass through the lines.

Despite the fact that both Lincoln and Lloyd were amateurs at the spy business, the plan worked so far as getting information to the president was concerned. The flow of valuable intelligence continued until the end of the war.

While Lloyd was suspected by the Confederates and arrested by them several times, he always managed to "wiggle through," as is evidenced by the fact that he, his wife, Nelly, and his assistant, Thomas H. S. Boyd, were even allowed to travel with President Davis and his cabinet when Davis fled Richmond in April of 1865. Lloyd and his party left the train at Danville, Virginia, and when Union forces under Maj. Gen. Horatio G. Wright entered Danville, Wright furnished them transportation to Washington.

There is a sad ending to Lloyd's story—typical, I might say, of the Lloyd family luck. After the war and broken in health as a result of the precarious existence he had lived, Lloyd filed a claim for his $200-a-month salary. He had had to destroy Mr. Lincoln's contract of employment when apprehended by the Confederates to keep that damaging document out of enemy hands. By the time he asked for his pay, Lincoln was dead, and there was no documentary contract in existence.

Lloyd died with the United States government owing him four years' salary. His widow brought suit; it was rejected by the court of claims. She appealed to the Supreme Court unsuccessfully.

Ironically (and this seems to be typical of bureaucracy in whatever era it functions), while the government refused to pay the salary Lloyd had been promised for his exceedingly hazardous job, it did reimburse him for the expenses he incurred. The ways of governments are "past finding out."

BOB LINCOLN BOWLING WHEN FATHER WON NOMINATION

Robert Todd Lincoln, the president's oldest son, then a prep school student in Exeter Academy had gone bowling while the Republican Convention was balloting on May 16, 1860. A friend, upon learning of Lincoln's nomination, hastened to find Bob at the bowling alley. Young Lincoln was concentratrating on his game when his friend ran in with the news of his father's nomination. "Good!" said Bob, slapping his hip. "I will have to write home for a check before he spends all his money on the campaign."

Learning of Lincoln's Death While in Andrew Johnson's Town

Hillborn C. Miller of Jackson, Ohio, a second lieutenant in Co. H., First Ohio Heavy Artillery, kept a diary during much of his service in the Civil War and tells of the troops hearing of the assassination of President Lincoln:

> On the 15th of April a part of our men were on the march between Jonesboro and Greenville. Here we heard of the assassination of Lincoln. Terrible news! But Garfield says "That the Government still lives." The writer went into Greenville on the 16th to load a train of wagons with supplies for the boys at Roane's Creek. One of our teamsters horse-whipped a citizen for saying Lincoln ought to have been killed; and this occurred on the same street and in sight of the sign "A. Johnson, tailor." who is to succeed Lincoln as President of the U.S., and where Gen. John Morgan was killed in Mrs. Williams' garden Sept. 4, 1864.
>
> In sorrow we trudge along, and out beyond Jonesboro we meet a portion of our regiment coming back from Roane's Creek. And taking an empty train of wagons went on to Roane's Creek for the ammunition and supplies of the Brigade, reporting there to Maj. Matthews on the 20th. The last battalion left there on the 21st and reached Greenville again on the 24th of April, 1865.

After the war, Lieutenant Miller returned to his home in Jackson, Ohio, where he married and entered business and politics, becoming probate judge of the county and siring, among other children, a daughter named Cora Anna, who, in 1893, married Homer A. Lloyd and, in 1901, did me the honor of becoming my mother.

114

Mr. Lincoln's Clothes

Contrary to general belief, Mr. Lincoln did not wear cheap clothing. His clothes were tailor-made and of good material. He wore white linen suits most of the time in summer and black broadcloth Prince Albert coats with matching vests and trousers the balance of the year. During his presidency, he wore the more formal black suits the year around and, so far as I have been able to learn, was not photographed wearing a white suit after he was elected president.

He wore boots instead of shoes and black ready-tied stocks instead of neckties. Most of the time he wore high silk hats and bought them from the Adam Hat Company.

Mr. Lincoln's tailor in Springfield was Benjamin R. Riddle. The custom seems to have been for Mr. Lincoln to purchase the cloth and trimmings and take them to Riddle, who would make the suit.

As an example is a transaction that took place on May 16, 1843. Mr. Lincoln went to Irvin's store and purchased enough cloth for a suit for $32.50. Material for trimming cost $3.87.

About that time, he also purchased three yards of cashmere cloth. Whether this was made into a suit or a garment for some member of the family is not indicated. Mrs. Lincoln was a very fine seamstress and made most of her own clothes and those of her children when they were small. It is possible that the cashmere cloth may have been for her.

About six months later, Mr. Lincoln purchased two and three-quarters yards of Beaver cloth, which was a heavy fabric of felted wool. He paid $9.50 to tailor Riddle for making the suit.

Some 300 of Mr. Lincoln's routine store purchases and personal financial transactions are preserved in the ledgers of John Irvin and Co. and Robert Irvin and Co., merchants of the Lincoln era in Springfield, and in the records of the Springfield Marine and Fire Insurance Company, which, in addition to writing insurance, conducted a banking business. Mr. Lincoln maintained a bank account with this firm.

OVERCOAT FOR
SECOND INAUGURATION:
SUIT WORN AT TIME
OF ASSASSINATION

I had often heard that Brooks Brothers, the New York clothiers, had made clothes for President Lincoln, and I wrote in July of 1975 asking if this was true.

Mr. Walter B. Stevens responded with the following:

CHAIRMAN   JUL 1   1975

Brooks Brothers
CLOTHING
Mens & Boys Furnishings, Hats & Shoes

NEW YORK
ATLANTA
BOSTON
CHICAGO
CINCINNATI
DETROIT
HOUSTON

LOS ANGELES
PITTSBURGH
SAN FRANCISCO
SCARSDALE
ST. LOUIS
WASHINGTON D. C.

346 MADISON AVE. COR. 44TH ST., NEW YORK, N. Y. 10017
MURRAY HILL 2-8800

New York, July 9th 1975

Mr. John A. Lloyd, Chairman
The Union Central Life Insurance Co.
Union Central Building
P. O. Box 179
Cincinnati, Ohio 45201

Dear Mr. Lloyd:

Most of our archives were inadvertantly destroyed shortly after World War II, but I will share with you what we have. The following is quoted from a booklet put out by Brooks Brothers on the occasion of its 125th Anniversary (1943):

"Generals Grant, Sheridan, Hooker and Sherman
were among our customers, but undoubtedly the
most illustrious was Abraham Lincoln, for whom
we made, among other things, an overcoat on the
occasion of his second inaugural. The quilted
lining of this was embellished (after the fashion
of those days) with an embroidered design of an
eagle holding in its beak a pennant inscribed
'One Country, one Destiny'.

This embroidery took two 10-hour days, on the
word transmitted to us in 1918 by the then
'more than 70 years young' woman who did it as
a girl. Her mother used to 'shrink duck and drilling'
for us in the 1860's 'as men in Summer time wore
suits of that material'."

I also enclose four newspaper articles concerning the
Brooks Brothers suit President Lincoln wore on the
night of his assassination. The suit was finally
purchased from the Smith family by some trucking
association and presented to the Ford Museum.

Regretfully, we have not records of sales or sizes,
but the latter might be supplied by the Ford Museum.

If we can be of any further assistance please advise.

                              Sincerely yours,

                              BROOKS BROTHERS

                              Walter B. Stevens
                              Walter B. Stevens
                              Director of Advertising

WBS:cb

enclosures

The Naming of Lincoln, Illinois

Mr. Lincoln had the distinction of having a city in Illinois named in his honor during his lifetime and *before* he became a national figure.

A group of landowners banded together to lay out a city about 25 miles north and slightly east of Springfield and along the right of way of the St. Louis, Alton and Chicago Railroad. They employed Mr. Lincoln as their lawyer, and in the course of his work in clearing titles to the land, plotting and laying out the town, drawing deeds, etc., they became such admiring friends, as well as clients, that when the time came to select a name, they chose that of their counsel. So the name Lincoln first appeared as a town on the map of the United States.

"I sought the Lord, and He heard me" (by Norman Vincent Peale)

Some years ago I had the privilege of holding for a few moments a copy of the Holy Bible that had been used by Abraham Lincoln in the White House during the darkest period of the Civil War. It was a big, old-fashioned Bible with an air of stability about it. My attention was directed to a passage that Lincoln evidently valued very highly. In the margin alongside it, there is a deeply dented, smudged place where the emancipator's finger must have rested repeatedly as he read.

The passage is the fourth verse of the 34th Psalm and it reads: "I sought the Lord, and He heard me, and delivered me from all my fears."

The Barber Plays a Trick on Mr. Lincoln

It takes but little to send me off posthaste to run down the truth about a newly heard or seen item about Mr. Lincoln, no matter how insignificant.

In the February 1977 issue of the prestigious British journal, *History Today*, I read the following item among letters from readers:

LINCOLN AND TAD

GENTLEMEN,

As an interested reader of History Today, and as an history buff in general and a Lincoln buff in particular, I must point out a glaring error of historical fact in your story on Horace Greeley in the September, 1976 issue of your fine magazine.

On page 572 the caption under the picture of Abraham Lincoln with his son, Tad, reads, 'Lincoln with his youngest son "Tad"', photographed in the late 1850s'. It is, in fact, a picture of Lincoln and his youngest son, Tad, but the photograph was definitely *not* taken 'in the late 1850s'.

The photograph was made during Lincoln's Presidential years which started with his inauguration in March of 1861 and ended with his assassination four years later in April of 1865. This fact is clearly discernible in the photograph. Abraham Lincoln grew a beard between the time he was elected President in November of 1860 and his inauguration in March of 1861. Further, at the time of his inauguration in March of 1861, he parted his hair on the *left* side. About halfway through his first term as President he changed the part of his hair to the *right* side. Therefore, this photograph could have only been made *after* he became President and *after* he changed the part of his hair—probably in 1863. If I am not mistaken the picture was taken about that time by the great Civil War photographer, Mathew Brady.

> Very truly yours,
> WILLIAM B. CONDIT
> *Garden City, L.I.,*
> *New York*

The dating of a Lincoln photograph by the test of prebeard or postbeard is standard procedure, and I agree with Mr. Condit's application of this test; but the statement that "about halfway through his first term as President he changed the part of his hair to the *right* side" is a "horse of another color." This to me was something never heard before.

All the study I have made of photographs, lithographs, and paintings of Mr. Lincoln led me to the firm conviction that from the beginning to the end of his life Mr. Lincoln—

boy and man—parted his unruly hair on the left side.

So I looked again at every picture of Mr. Lincoln I had, both unbound and bookbound. Steven Lorant, in his magnificent work on Lincoln pictures, on pages 208–212 of the Bonanza revised edition, 1975, second printing, 1976, shows photographs of Lincoln with his hair parted on the *right* side of his head. These are reproduced on pages 323 and 324.

These pictures showing the hair parted on the right side were taken in Brady's Washington gallery by one of Brady's assistants, Anthony Berger on February 9, 1864.

Since all photographs before and after the sitting of February 4, 1864, show the hair parted on the left side, why was it parted on the right side that day? Was the president experimenting? Had Mrs. Lincoln suggested the change in some fancy that it improved his appearance? Was it a case of an inverted plate in printing?

Curator James T. Hickey of the Lincoln Collection in Springfield, Illinois, solved the mystery.

Yes. Mr. Lincoln's hair was parted on the right side on that one day of his life.

No, Mr. Lincoln hadn't done it.

Well, how did it happen?

But let Mr. Hickey tell the story. I quote him:

Frank B. Carpenter, the artist, was present the day, February 9, 1864, when Antony Berger took the seven photographs of Lincoln. On the back of one of the photographs, Carpenter wrote, "His barber by mistake this day for some unaccountable reason, parted the hair on the President's right side, instead of his left."

On April 20, 1864, when Berger made another photograph the part of the hair was back on the left side.

And that clears up the mystery. *History Today*'s correspondent was in error when he wrote, "About halfway through his term as President he changed the part of his hair to his *right* side" and also when he added that he thought the picture was taken by Mathew Brady.

Mr. Lincoln never changed the way *he* parted his hair.

So ends an excursion into what all but Lincoln "buffs" will call trivia but what a seeker after fact will recognize as an effort at accuracy about a man of whom too much inaccuracy has been written and spoken time and time again.

Immortality

At 7:21 on the morning of April 15, 1865 Abraham Lincoln died, the victim of an assassin's bullet.

When the last breath had been drawn, Secretary of War Stanton said either "now he belongs to the ages" or "now he belongs to the angels." Which of these sentiments Stanton uttered really makes no difference. The substance is that immortality had begun for Abraham Lincoln.

Contemplation of his life and works reveals the utter simplicity of this unusual man of manifold talents and monolithic dedication, a man whose vision of the totality of the greatest crisis our nation ever faced was so clear and so complete. He saw it developing and diagnosed its causes accurately two decades before it burst, with terror and destruction and death upon the disbelieving nation. He saw with absolute accuracy and acted with tenacious, single-minded purpose. And under every circumstance, his character never varied. His uncomplicated spirit never gave way to delusions of grandeur, to arrogance, to egocentric love of glory, or to passion for power.

And these thoughts lead me to wonder what was the underlying fundamental attribute of his character?

What is the answer to this question: why, almost 111 years after his death, do the people not only of the United States but of the entire world study and ponder and explore and venerate the life of Abraham Lincoln?

Thirty-eight men have occupied the office of the presidency since our republic was founded. All but three of them are dead. A half dozen seem to stand out above the others: Washington, the founding chief, whom Henry Lee described in his eloquent eulogy in 1799 as being "first in war, first in peace, first in the hearts of his countrymen"; Jefferson, who is perhaps remembered for his political philosophy more than for his presidency, of which the most lasting contributions now appear to have been the Louisiana Purchase and the Lewis and Clark expedition; Jackson, the swashbuckling commoner who smashed the Bank of the United States and revised the monetary system; the Roosevelts: Theodore, who consummated the McKinley conquests and made America a world power, and Franklin, who changed completely the sociological and commercial complexion of the country and set the stage for the ascendancy of minority racial domination. And Abraham Lincoln.

These are the most written about, the most talked about, the most often portrayed in film, in television, on radio, and on stage. Some persons may wish to delete one or the other of the presidents in my list and substitute or add their own preferences, and I would not quibble with them.

But make this test: ask a score of the men and women you know to write down the names of the half-dozen greatest presidents of the United States, and you will get a variety of answers, but on every list you will find the name of Abraham Lincoln.

Ask your foreign friends to name the ten greatest figures of world history in the last two hundred years, and on every list you will find the name of Abraham Lincoln.

Why? Why Lincoln?

That question has been challenging me through all the years since I first became interested in Lincoln.

Why does Lincoln tower above them all?

I received a letter not long ago from a friend in Jackson, Mississippi, who had read the little book on Lincoln that I wrote under the imprimatur of the Queen City Optimists Club, and she put this proposition to me: "Would you consider doing a summary of your conclusions on the man you have so thoroughly studied; to tie it all together?"

And isn't that just another way of asking: why Lincoln?

Is it his clarity of expression that certainly eclipses that of any other statesman of his era or of the preceding or ensuing years?

Is it his genius as an executive—and he was great in this field—so much so that he could make effective leaders of a strange assortment of cabinet ministers who were exceedingly jealous of each other but who, under his inspiration, gave strong leadership to a young republic, rent by fratricidal strife?

Is it because this peaceable lawyer, faced with ruinous political generalship in his army, was forced to become a military strategist, himself, and became a master of the basic principles of the science of war?

Is it because this man, whose employees never numbered more than a bevy of law students clerking in his office and a hired man and a hired girl, learned the science of the selection of men so well that he could come up with a Grant and a Sherman and a Sheridan to bring about the victory his country had to have to survive?

None of these attributes could be spared from the leadership that the nation and the cause that Lincoln led had to have, but other Americans have communicated well with people; others have been great generals and great executives; yet none survives as a spiritual and intellectual force as does Lincoln.

There is some other spark in the Lincoln character that no other man in his era possessed. What is it?

Is there a clue in the humility and simplicity and directness of the man I described in the incidents recited earlier in this chapter?

No, I think we must seek further for the answer.

Why have more books been written about Lincoln than any other American, perhaps than any other human being? Why is he so often quoted? Why is he so definitely an influence so long after his death?

Jay Monaghan, in his Lincoln Bibliography, published back in 1945 (31 years ago), listed 3,958 books and pamphlets written about Lincoln up to that time, and the output in the ensuing years has shown no diminution; it probably has more than doubled.

Will we find the answer to "Why Lincoln?" if we mine that great paper mass sheet by sheet—thousands of them—and word by word—millions of them? Will the secret of Lincoln's greatness and his unusual appeal begin to appear? I am trying, and I can find many reasons for his greatness, but these myriad pages have not yet given up the answer to my question.

So much of this mass of words is legend, told and retold, myth repeated over and over. But remember this, Lincoln the myth and Lincoln the legend would have died the death that fictional and fanciful accounts deserve long, long ago. It is the real, earthy Lincoln who is immortal, not the legendary so-called martyr. We must seek the answer in what we can prove to be true in and about his life.

Somewhere in his humble, honest reality, in the breadth of his intellect, in the courage and stamina of his character, and in the deep recesses of his soul lies the answer to the enigmatic question "Why Lincoln?"

So baffled have I been by this question that I have read and searched for the answer and was about to abandon hope of finding it when, suddenly, while seeking information on an entirely different subject, I came across an incident in Sacred Writ that I believe reveals the secret.

In the story of the calling by Jesus of men to be his disciples, it is told how Peter and James and John and Bartholomew came to be enlisted; then, an entirely different reason for selection flashes across the page when Nathaniel is chosen. This is how it is written: "Jesus saw Nathaniel coming and saith to him: behold an Israelite, indeed, in whom there is no guile!"

My dictionaries define the word "guile" as craft, deceit, cunning, duplicity, treachery.

And the thought came to me: here I have found the answer to my question "Why Lincoln?" But to be certain, the search could not be complete until it took another turn. I began deliberately and carefully to try to find in the story of Lincoln's years, in his speeches and in his acts, evidence of guile. And in a more than cursory study I can find no act or even a phrase revealing craft, deceit, or hypocrisy, cunning, duplicity or treachery.

The same threads of truth and honesty and integrity and realism run through his every utterance from youth to death. There is no cant or braggadocio or breast beating to the "I am honest" theme anywhere to be found. The pure gold of his integrity is there throughout his life, but he not only never told of it, I doubt if he ever realized it. It was just the way he was.

We are used to being deceived by rulers. Today, presidents and premiers and dictators and cabinet officers and legislators all over the world, including our United States, practice deceit on their people. Governments are just not to be believed anymore on any score.

But Lincoln could always be believed; and because people could believe him, they believed in him, and they believe in him to this very day.

And that, I believe, is why Lincoln towers above them all, why he will live forever in memory and in history as the one man who never deceived his people, who never practiced the modern maneuver of the credibility gap. That is the answer to the question "Why Lincoln?"

He literally was a man in whom there was no guile.

How America could be transformed into the great America of which Lincoln dreamed and for which he toiled if only our beneficent God would give us once more a leader "in whom there is no guile."